GO FIGURE!

Lesley S. J. Farmer

1999
Teacher Ideas Press
A Division of
Libraries Unlimited, Inc.
Englewood, Colorado

Copyright © 1999 Lesley S. J. Farmer
All Rights Reserved

No part of this publication may be reproduced, stored in a retrieval system, or transmitted, in any form or by any means, electronic, mechanical, photocopying, recording, or otherwise, without the prior written permission of the publisher. An exception is made for individual librarians and educators, who may make copies of activity sheets for classroom use in a single school or library. Standard citation information should appear on each page.

TEACHER IDEAS PRESS
A Division of
Libraries Unlimited, Inc.
P.O. Box 6633
Englewood, CO 80155-6633
1-800-237-6124
www.lu.com/tip

Library of Congress Cataloging-in-Publication Data

Farmer, Lesley S. J.
   Go figure! : mathematics through sports / Lesley S.J. Farmer.
   xiv, 171 p. 22x28 cm.
   Includes bibliographical references and index.
   ISBN 1-56308-708-1 (softbound)
   1. Mathematics. I. Title.
QA39.2.F373 1999
510--dc21   99-33172
                                                                         CIP

*DEDICATED
to*

*My Mother
who taught me that math was a game*

and to

*David Loertscher
who started me in the book publishing game
and gave me this idea*

Contents

Preface xiii

Part I: Introduction 1
    Math Power 3
        Why Math? 3
        The Way We Were 3
        The Way Kids Learn 4
        Goals for Powerful Math Students 5
        Curricular Standards and Strands 6
        Assessment 7
        Instructional Design and Implementation 8
        Mathematics as Process 9
        What Teachers Need to Know 11
        The Role of Information Literacy 12
        Teaching Math Using Sports Training Techniques 13
    Framework for Math Units 15
        Workout/Marathon Template 16
            Teacher Play Book 16
            Warm-Ups 16
            Student Game Plan 17

Part II: Body Works 19
    How Do You Measure Up? 21
        Teacher Play Book 21
        Warm-Ups 22
        Student Game Plan 23
            Dugout 24
    Where's the Perfect Body? 25
        Teacher Play Book 25
        Warm-Ups 26
        Student Game Plan 27
            Dugout 28
    Let Me Measure the Ways 29
        Teacher Play Book 29
        Warm-Ups 30
        Student Game Plan 31
            Dugout 32
    Composing a Body 33
        Teacher Play Book 33
        Warm-Ups 34
        Student Game Plan 35
            Dugout 36

Part II: Body Works (*continued*)
    Emergency Systems 37
        Teacher Play Book...37
        Warm-Ups 39
        Student Game Plan 40
        Dugout..41
    Marathon: Body Morph 42
        Teacher Play Book...42
        Student Game Plan 43
        Dugout..43

Part III: Be All That You Can Be...45
    You Are What You Eat 47
        Teacher Play Book...47
        Warm-Ups 48
        Student Game Plan 49
        Dugout..50
    The Bouncing Ball of Weight 51
        Teacher Play Book...51
        Warm-Ups 52
        Student Game Plan 54
        Dugout..55
    The Body Machine 56
        Teacher Play Book...56
        Warm-Ups 57
        Student Game Plan 58
        Dugout..59
    Getting Pumped 60
        Teacher Play Book...60
        Warm-Ups 61
        Student Game Plan 62
        Dugout..63
    Oh, My Aching Back! 64
        Teacher Play Book...64
        Warm-Ups 65
        Student Game Plan 66
        Dugout..66
    Marathon: Go for the Gold! 67
        Teacher Play Book...67
        Student Game Plan 68
        Dugout..68

Part IV: Knowing the Ropes...69
    Knowing Your Limits 71
        Teacher Play Book...71
        Warm-Ups 72
        Student Game Plan 73
        Dugout..73

What's the Score? 74
    Teacher Play Book 74
    Warm-Ups 75
    Student Game Plan 76
        Dugout 77

Collide Scope 78
    Teacher Play Book 78
    Warm-Ups 79
    Student Game Plan 80
        Dugout 80

Projecting Yourself 81
    Teacher Play Book 81
    Warm-Ups 82
    Student Game Plan 83
        Dugout 83

What a Drag! 84
    Teacher Play Book 84
    Warm-Ups 85
    Student Game Plan 86
        Dugout 87

Going in Circles 88
    Teacher Play Book 88
    Warm-Ups 89
    Student Game Plan 90
        Dugout 90

Friction Feat 91
    Teacher Play Book 91
    Warm-Ups 92
    Student Game Plan 93
        Dugout 93

What a Racquet! 94
    Teacher Play Book 94
    Warm-Ups 95
    Student Game Plan 96
        Dugout 96

Marathon: The Story of a Hit 97
    Teacher Play Book 97
    Warm-Ups 98
    Student Game Plan 99
        Dugout 99

Part V: Playing the Odds 101

Record Breaking 103
- Teacher Play Book 103
- Warm-Ups 104
- Student Game Plan 105
  - Dugout 105

Battle of the Sexes 106
- Teacher Play Book 106
- Warm-Ups 107
- Student Game Plan 108
  - Dugout 108

Playing Against Yourself 109
- Teacher Play Book 109
- Warm-Ups 110
- Student Game Plan 111
  - Dugout 112

Kill the Umpire 113
- Teacher Play Book 113
- Warm-Ups 114
- Student Game Plan 115
  - Dugout 115

Timing Is Everything 116
- Teacher Play Book 116
- Warm-Ups 117
- Student Game Plan 118
  - Dugout 118

A Hard Combination to Beat 119
- Teacher Play Book 119
- Warm-Ups 120
- Student Game Plan 121
  - Dugout 121

What's Your Playing Level? 122
- Teacher Play Book 122
- Warm-Ups 123
- Student Game Plan 124
  - Dugout 124

Playing Your Part 125
- Teacher Play Book 125
- Warm-Ups 126
- Student Game Plan 127
  - Dugout 127

Marathon: Dream Teams 128
    Teacher Play Book...128
    Warm-Ups 129
    Student Game Plan 130
        Dugout..130

Part VI: Sports for (Fun and) Profit...131

The Independent Spirit 133
    Teacher Play Book...133
    Warm-Ups 134
    Student Game Plan 135
        Dugout..135

For the Love of the Game 136
    Teacher Play Book...136
    Warm-Ups 137
    Student Game Plan 138
        Dugout..139

Fit for Business 140
    Teacher Play Book...140
    Warm-Ups 141
    Student Game Plan 142
        Dugout..142

Cities and Franchises:
  A Marriage Made in Heaven? 143
    Teacher Play Book...143
    Warm-Ups 144
    Student Game Plan 145
        Dugout..145

It Takes a Village
  to Put on a Sports Event 146
    Teacher Play Book...146
    Warm-Ups 147
    Student Game Plan 148
        Dugout..148

It Pays to Win 149
    Teacher Play Book...149
    Warm-Ups 150
    Student Game Plan 151
        Dugout..151

It's All in the Cards 152
    Teacher Play Book...152
    Warm-Ups 153
    Student Game Plan 154
        Dugout..155

The Gambling Life	156
Teacher Play Book	156
Warm-Ups	157
Student Game Plan	158
Dugout	158
Marathon: Is Sports in Your Future?	159
Teacher Play Book	159
Warm-Ups	160
Student Game Plan	161
Dugout	161
Bibliography	163
Math	163
Anatomy and Fitness	163
Science	164
Sports	164
Instruction	165
Index	167
About the Author	171

Preface

Math is all around us: the day's temperature, the stock market, packaging, time, taxes, and even death. From flower arrangements to prom arrangements, from the ozone layer to Mach 1, we are practically bombarded by math.

Yet many people say that they're "hopeless at math" or have math phobia. Girls, in particular, may lament, "I've never been good with numbers." Even more sadly, listeners may respond by saying, "I wasn't either" or "Don't worry, you'll never need it." Remember the movie *Peggy Sue Got Married*? The 28-year-old heroine is transported back to high school, and exclaims during the middle of an algebra test, "I never had to use algebra since I got out of school!" Maybe not consciously, but if she ever shopped, changed a recipe, or did her income tax, then Peggy Sue owed a debt of gratitude to her algebra teacher.

The truth is, people would never stand for this kind of withering excuse if the skill were reading. What causes this difference? Part of it may be due to the abstractness of the subject: the mysterious "x." Part may stem from negative experiences memorizing algorithms by rote, such as the manual way to find square root. Part may stem from book-centered instruction or word problems that had no meaning to the learner. Much has to do with the unconscious way we deal with math. Think of the people who keep scorecards in their heads. Consider how people figure out ways to pack the car or the refrigerator efficiently. Think of people troubleshooting computers. Shall we point to clever ways in which people hide income from the IRS? All these skills involve math, but they might not have been acknowledged in school.

Yet the working world does realize the need for mathematical literacy. The 1991 SCANS report notes the need for basic mathematical skills, problem-solving ability, and the means to process information and think systematically. On the basis of technology alone, mathematical thinking is crucial in order to survive economically. In today's world, math is a definite "should."

Now consider sports. It too is a lifelong activity; children's play is vital for coordination and basic social skills. As for adults, the interest in sports is palpable for many. Municipal bonds are passed to build sports stadiums. Millions of dollars are spent on advertisements during the Super Bowl. A million French people gathered along the Champs Elysées to celebrate their 1998 Coupe du Monde win. Besides the large core of sports participants, from volleyball to speed-skating, most people watch sports at least occasionally. Even the sports phobic usually takes a peak at an Olympic game result, or listens to the Monday morning sports commentary at the office. And at the center of this sports phenomenon is math.

One of the keys to lifelong use and appreciation of math is early practice and success. Although girls still take fewer advanced courses in math than boys do, they are more likely to try if they have an early solid grounding in math. When students can see the applications of math to the real world, they stay more engaged. When they can actively explore concepts mathematically and talk about them, students make connections more creatively. When math builds upon students' interests, teachers see more student progress.

This book, then, brings these two notions together: sports and mathematics. Educators can use sports to "hook" the student, providing a real-life context based on student interest. Not only do students become aware of mathematical thinking, but they can be "trained" to improve their mathematical skills and habits of mind through sports-related learning experiences in math.

It should also be noted that the author has a second agenda: to foster student information literacy. The answers aren't in the book. Even the data upon which to derive an answer are often outside the text. Why? Because math lies in the real world; we need to locate, gather, and sift complex data from a variety of sources. This step may seem like a bothersome and time-consuming addition to the learning experience, but it helps students contextualize their exploration and make it more authentic. Likewise, the assessment of such work can be much more realistic and valuable. Such practice reflects current pedagogical thinking: students learn in-depth through engagement in cross-disciplinary, thematic, real-world-based educational experiences. Math then connects with different ways of thinking and manipulating information and so becomes more meaningful.

Part 1 of the book deals with "math power": contemporary mathematical education. Based on the 1989 National Council of Teachers of Mathematics document on school mathematics curriculum, it explains how to structure educational experiences to help students think and communicate, drawing on mathematical ideas and using mathematical tools and techniques. A special note for librarians concludes this part, which shows how to use reference tools to help students gather and process sports and math data.

Most of the book is composed of units that explore mathematical concepts using a meaningful sports context. Five major topics are covered, each with its own mathematical focus. Within each topic, units are arranged from single-concept exercises (warm-ups) to extensive open-ended projects (marathons). A lesson template notes the mathematical strand, sport, and information skill. The physiology unit focuses on measurement. The training unit focuses on functions. The third unit, how to play the game, highlights geometry. The sports competition unit focuses on statistics. The last unit examines sports economics, emphasizing data representation.

Time to "hit" the book—and play ball—mathematically!

Part I

Introduction

Math Power

How can educators help students become competent and enthusiastic about mathematics? This chapter explores the current thought on the mathematics curriculum, and discusses the need for providing context-rich, complex learning experiences that encourage students to think creatively about mathematics. It also shows how sports can motivate students and anchor mathematics in real-life settings.

WHY MATH?

Why is mathematics so important in academic preparation? Basically, it provides analytical tools for representing things and finding relationships between them. Usually those representations are abstract, be it a model, symbol, or diagram. Often those concepts constitute part of a structure that is either self-evident or becomes apparent after mathematical investigation. As part of the process, these structures and relationships need to be tested and verified; mathematics, like other sciences, is built upon the notion of hypothesis and evidence to support a conclusion.

Indeed, mathematics supports scientific habits of mind: respect for evidence and logic, a healthy balance of openness to new evidence and objective skepticism of quick claims, the use of tools to measure and otherwise manipulate numbers and other mathematical constructs, an ability to make realistic estimations and predictions based on available data, and the capacity to communicate these ways of thinking.

Although mathematics enjoys the freedom of abstraction and an appreciation of theory for its own intellectual and esthetic sake, it is soundly grounded in the everyday and offers a universal way to find patterns in the world in order to improve that world. No wonder mathematics was considered part of philosophy and a mainstay in classical education. No wonder, in these days of electronics and virtual reality, it remains the queen of science.

THE WAY WE WERE

Readin', writin', and 'rithmetic. Times tables, formulas, worksheets. Hopefully, not anymore. While all of these competencies remain important, the approach to mastering them has changed over the years. Mathematics, in particular, had the educational image of rote learning. Each class period was the same: the teacher would review homework, lecture from the book about the new concept/formula, work problems on the board, and assign the night's homework (with a test on Friday). For high school, curriculum was also lockstep: algebra, geometry, algebra II/trigonometry, pre-calculus (or calculus for the "smart" students). "Dumb" students took business math or accounting. The times are changing.

That system did work for some students: abstract thinkers, sequential learners, field-independent processors, visual and aural learners, independent workers, those who had experience with the word problem world, and those who went through the paces in order to get into the college of their choice. But what about the other students?

More important, how well did those students learn mathematics? Was there short-term or long-term retention? Could students explain the logic and reasoning behind the concepts? Could they apply it to their lives during and after the course? Could they connect mathematical concepts with other courses or situations? Did they like math?

THE WAY KIDS LEARN

Advances in educational research have concluded that several factors increase student achievement and improve student attitude toward academics in general and mathematics in particular.

First, educators have to get the students' attention. Each child needs to be "hooked" on a personal level. It may be curiosity, intellectual connection, emotional identification, or even peer pressure. But the student must somehow become aware of the ideas to be introduced and explored.

Second, students must become engaged. They must interact with the resources provided or available in their environment in order to manipulate the information, interpret it, synthesize it, use it. They need to connect with other people—their peers, their teachers, their friends or family—in order to share their insights and test their conclusions. Ultimately, they need to interact with the world to apply their learning or to test it in real-life situations.

Indeed, authenticity is a key factor for establishing mathematical "rapport." Teachers can help students connect the topic at hand with other coursework as well as with daily life and personal interests. Connections with prior work also offer continuity so students can build on existing knowledge and strengths and look forward to upcoming topics. Part of this connection extends to language arts; students need the opportunity to communicate their thinking and logical arguments, to use linguistic symbols to complement mathematical systems. The mathematics activity itself should resemble or call upon real-world situations and resources. Moreover, the assessment should be aligned with the instruction and activity and, therefore, be authentic. A portfolio delineating the mathematical problem, the approach, the evidence, and the reasoning leading to the solution provides a much richer picture of a student's knowledge than a multiple-guess test — and it facilitates easier transfer of learning to other contexts.

To accomplish these goals, the experience should be designed with the learner as the center of focus. Knowledge is limited if not used, and it is most likely to be useful if it relates to the learner. Thus, rather than focusing on the intricacies of a mathematical proof, a teacher would be more effective spending time on developing a learning environment in which students could explore those intricacies for themselves. Such an environment needs to be filled with intriguing stimuli and access to relevant resources. The physical space needs to be flexible to accommodate different types of learners and different ways to explore mathematics. The setting needs to feel safe or respectful for students so they can take intellectual risks without fear of negative academic consequences. There needs to be adequate time to "do" mathematics as well as to reflect on it; alternative times and methods should also be available for those students who need it. Most important, the teacher needs to help students identify their own interests and academic needs and facilitate ways to help them build on their strengths and meet those needs by asking probing questions, suggesting sources, offering useful heuristics, providing meaningful contexts, and encouraging students to be independent thinkers.

For the learning environment to work, an underlying principle must be believed and put into action: that all students can learn. For this kind of inclusion to become a reality, the teacher must have high expectations for all students and seek ways for students to meet those expectations. Obviously, the teacher needs a strong repertoire of teaching and learning strategies in order to accomplish this feat. The following are some specific techniques for students with different kinds of intelligences:

Issue	Strategy
Linguistic	Write word problems and reflections
Kinesthetic	Use manipulatives, act out word problems, measure
Spatial	Draw pictures and graphs, create models
Interpersonal	Work collaboratively, use simulations, peer coach
Intrapersonal	Reflect on math, self-pace work
Musical	Look for patterns and rhythms, create math "raps"

As most teachers know, a variety of methods provide change and spark a sense of novelty for students. Of course, some students need routine and are easily distracted, so a core of predictable behaviors and a quiet corner can help provide a calm atmosphere while offering options for the class. Guide sheets and other specific learning accommodations can help those students with special needs participate with the rest of the class, making them feel included.

GOALS FOR POWERFUL MATH STUDENTS

The National Council of Teachers of Mathematics (NCTM) carefully examined mathematics education for grades K–12 in light of current research, practice, and needs. As a result, their 1989 document, *Curriculum and Evaluation Standards for School Mathematics*, was a significant reform effort to provide a broad framework for school mathematics that would prepare students over the next decade. Their intention is to help students use mathematics with confidence, solve problems, reason and communicate mathematically, and value math. In other words, it's not enough to plug in a number to calculate a circle's circumference; a student should be able to demonstrate how that formula was derived and its implications in other contexts. This is powerful learning, and it exemplifies the basic tenets of NCTM's draft 1999 process standards: problem-solving, reasoning, mathematical connections, communication, and representation.

This radical view of mathematics, in light of "back to basics" philosophy, tries to get at the conceptual underpinnings of mathematics so students can use a repertoire of analytical tools to solve problems in real life. Certainly, most situations are not textbook "clean" with controlled figures; building a home, starting a business, and training for competition are complex issues and require intricate mathematical connections. Thus, school experience in mathematics should mirror some of this complexity.

The California Department of Education examined NCTM's efforts, and translated its goals into a basic philosophy that "mathematically powerful students think and communicate, drawing on mathematical ideas and using mathematical tools and techniques." Within this pedagogical construct, mathematical ideas are complex, meaningful, and multidimensional. Students are expected to put effort into their thinking and self-regulate their progress. On their parts, educators need to communicate high expectations for all students and give them opportunities to learn individually and collaboratively. Other states reinforce this philosophy of mathematics education for youth.

Some real-life goals have also shaped state and organizational perspectives on mathematics education. The public wants students to become critical consumers, so they need to be able to calculate and estimate accurately. Citizens need to make good decisions, so students need to be able to design critical questions, represent information meaningfully, and draw conclusions based on evidence. Industry wants good problem-solvers and producers, so students need to learn how to manipulate ideas and objects, creating models and other means to design solutions. Business also expects employees to manage, interpret, and improve systems, so students need to analyze systems critically and objectively. Adults need to plan and organize, so students need to practice managing time and resources. Finally, people need to recognize that more than one answer exists, so students need to see that reality in their mathematical experiences as well.

CURRICULAR STANDARDS AND STRANDS

Along with these broad principles and beliefs, the NCTM realizes that specific competencies need to be addressed. In the past, particularly in high school, the day-by-day curriculum was pretty much standardized (maybe calcified). Replacing this somewhat arbitrary lockstep, the NCTM has posited mathematical strands and unifying ideas that cross some grades. With these foci, students explore problems contextually. The curriculum for grades 6 through 12 includes:

- problem solving
- communication
- reasoning and proof
- connections
- representation
- number and operation
- patterns, functions, and algebra
- data analysis, statistics, and probability
- geometry and spatial sense
- measurement

Grades 9 through 12 have the same strands, but they are explored at a more sophisticated level.

The first five points undergird mathematical habits of mind. The remaining concepts are more content-specific. It should be noted that they are not treated autonomously, though. For instance, when students take a survey of class heights, they are learning about number relationships, measurement, computation, statistics, and possibly patterns. Though the teacher may highlight one mathematical idea, that idea does not exist in a vacuum; it is contextually approached.

Transcending standards, NCTM has proposed guiding principles that they think are vital for sound educational practice. Furthermore, NCTM asserts that having these principles in place will optimize student success rate. The six principles follow:

- Equity: all students should have high-quality mathematical programs.
- Curriculum: mathematical content should be coherent and comprehensive.
- Teaching: teachers should be caring and competent.
- Learning: programs should make sure that all students understand and use mathematics.
- Technology: technology should be incorporated in order to help students understand and apply mathematics in the real world.
- Assessment: assessment should be used throughout the program to monitor, enhance and evaluate mathematical practice of both students and teachers.

ASSESSMENT

NCTM asserts that all students can learn this mathematical curriculum. Although some differentiation may be made for high school course sequencing because some students lack the prerequisite skills or take longer to learn concepts, and some students may take college courses such as Advanced Placement calculus, teachers are encouraged to group students heterogeneously and cover the same concepts with all of them. Differentiation arises because students have various strengths and needs. Individual backgrounds, interests, and learning styles also need to be acknowledged and embraced because they provide a richer context for learning. Thus, if students are exploring nutrition, different eating habits can be shared and small groups can take advantage of linguistic, computational, visual, and organizational strengths of their teammates. The teacher then acts as a sideline coach, helping students through rough spots or accommodating those with special needs. Those students who excel may be encouraged to challenge themselves through more in-depth exploration of the problem or through related enrichment activities.

With this kind of inclusivity comes more complex assessment; multiple-choice tests or even simple problem sheets do not do justice to students' acquisition of skills and ability to transfer learning. Rather, students need to demonstrate their learning through articulate communication both linguistically and mathematically. For a given unit, students could identify the problem, state their hypothesis, explain their approach, trace their mathematical thinking, show their solution, and present a solid argument based on the evidence gathered and manipulated. In other cases, students might present a portfolio of work, create a mathematical model, or even design their own activity demonstrating their knowledge. What keeps the assessment from being overwhelming is a consistent focus on the important concepts and a balance among skills, concepts, and reasoning abilities.

It becomes apparent that the assessment must be aligned with the instruction, and be useful to both the students and the teacher. Because assessment should help guide instruction, it should be formative as well as summative. Obviously, assessment should measure student learning fairly, examining student understanding and strategies of the activity at hand. It has been said that a student's verbal explanation tells more about a student's linguistic skill than about his or her mathematical skill, but the teacher should help all students become articulate mathematical communicators.

One means to ensure equity in assessment is to use *rubrics:* descriptions of student performance at different levels of competencies. Students should know these rubrics ahead of time so their efforts will be aligned with the desired outcomes. A general rubric may be applied to all activities, such as:

4: Fully accomplishes the purpose of the task
3: Substantially accomplishes the purpose of the task
2: Partially accomplishes the purpose of the task
1: Little or no progress toward accomplishing the purpose of the task

Each level would be detailed in terms of grasping mathematical concepts, using the concepts, and recording the process. Each aspect would be assessed separately so students and teachers would know which parts need additional work. More specific rubrics may be designed to particularize those ideas that are highlighted in one unit, rather like underlining or excerpting one part of a text. It is obvious, though, that process as well as product is to be validated.

INSTRUCTIONAL DESIGN AND IMPLEMENTATION

Because mathematics instruction is no longer limited to the textbook, teachers need to spend more time establishing an effective overall learning environment as well as designing specific mathematical learning experiences. Basically, teachers bring mathematics and students together. Like a good host, teachers must set the scene for successful encounters. Teachers need to start with the child. What are the individual's interests, strengths, and needs? What prerequisite skills does he or she have? What adolescent/preadolescent developmental qualities need to be considered? What will engage the child? All of these questions help to define the appropriate mathematical tasks.

The other part of the instructional equation is the mathematical content. A number of critical questions need to be addressed:

1. What concepts have been previously explored, and in what way and to what depth?
2. What strands will be emphasized?
3. How does the present unit fit into the total math curriculum?

4. What instruction is needed to set up the student activity?
5. What tasks best allow students to examine the mathematics?
6. What resources are needed and available for students to accomplish their task?
7. What physical and group arrangement provides the richest experience?
8. What time frame allows for sufficient investigation yet maintains a good pace?
9. What learning outcomes are expected?
10. How will students be assessed?

Designing units can seem like a daunting job, which is why teachers need to work collaboratively with others and consult outside resources in order to structure class time effectively.

MATHEMATICS AS PROCESS

Several mathematical procedures may be considered "standard equipment" for mathematical inquiry. Therefore, part of the students' learning activity must include instruction in using these standard practices as tools to analyze data.

Polya's seminal book *How to Solve It* (1988) offers a systematic way to approach a variety of mathematical problems:

1. Understand the problem: what is unknown, what data exist? What is the condition?
2. Devise a plan: connect the data with the unknown, consider related problems, plan a way to solve the problem.
3. Carry out the plan: check and verify each step.
4. Analyze the solution: check the result and argument, consider other approaches, transfer the method to other problems.

Design briefs, a recent term used to help students examine a problem, correlates well with Polya's mathematical insights. Typically used in technology education, this teaching tool engages students in a contextual problem, and then guides them in formulating their own solutions through challenge, objectives, resources, evaluation, and application. This structure can be used particularly with open-ended math activities.

Several heuristics suggest specific ways to plan a solution. As teachers work with students to examine mathematics, they should point out these techniques as mathematical strategies that can be applied to other problems — with an eye to using them in other disciplines as well. The common ones include:

- Drawing a picture or diagram
- Exploring special cases, such as zero or one
- Simplifying the problem: breaking it down into simpler single steps
- Modifying the problem: changing a condition or data

With NCTM's emphasis on active learning, several interactive processes have been used in current math discovery. Fortunately, these processes are often used in other disciplines so students have another opportunity to make mathematical connections with the rest of their studies. Following are some examples that encourage engaged student investigation.

Surveys. Surveys are an increasingly acceptable way to gather data, and students enjoy the process. Both qualitative and quantitative mathematical relationships can be discovered through the use of surveys.

1. Students need to determine the mathematical reason—the goal—for their survey.
2. They must develop a series of questions, which should be pilot-tested for clarity and objectivity.
3. They must decide whom to survey — and by whom; in some cases, students need to grapple with sampling vs. population implications.
4. Students must then plan and carry out their survey: what form it will take, how to administer it, what permissions are needed, what time frame will be required, what controls can be maintained.
5. Students need to organize and represent their data; carrying out this task is simplified if the plan for such documentation is made when the survey itself is being developed.
6. Students then need to find meaningful patterns that synthesize the data, transforming it into a useful mathematical relationship.
7. Only then can they make logical conclusions and arguments about their survey results.

Experiments. Experiments demonstrate the classical scientific method, and point out the fact that mathematics is a science in itself. Experiments are particularly useful when discussing correlations and functions.

1. Students determine their hypothesis based on their first encounter with the problem.
2. Based on the hypothesis, they set up the experiment after determining the variables, controls, and resources.
3. Students need to determine what to measure and how; in some cases, they must put in a factor for growth or other change over time.
4. Once they gather the data, students can then analyze it mathematically.

Games. Gaming theory has become popular — and practically a necessity in business. At its simplest, though, games examine the function of rules on predicting outcomes. Students enjoy the prospect that their early childhood pastimes have grown-up applications and sophistication.

1. For any game, students first have to understand the game: its objectives and rules.
2. At this point, they can make predictions about a game's outcome, which form their hypothesis.

3. Students test their predictions by playing the game and gathering data about it (the key to the mathematical aspect of the process).

4. They can discover the winner and determine the mathematical reason for the outcome.

5. Optionally, students can change a rule and predict/test the "new" outcome.

Monte Carlo simulations. Typically introduced in higher mathematics, this process shows how a sampling can be used to model or "test run" a complex mathematical relationship.

1. Presented with the problem, students conjecture what will happen.

2. They model the problem by determining the critical features and simulating them.

3. They then run trials on the model and collect the findings.

4. Students synthesize the data into meaningful patterns.

5. Based on the mathematical relationships uncovered, students analyze the outcome and predict how the actual problem would be played out.

WHAT TEACHERS NEED TO KNOW

Such a complex array of instructional issues requires significant teacher expertise: of mathematics, of instruction, of learning, and of student behavior. Deep mathematical knowledge is crucial; teachers need to see the connections among concepts and keys to accessing them by students. A seemingly straightforward student survey carries with it profound statistical ramifications; teachers need to know to what degree students can handle sophisticated mathematics. Likewise, teachers need to be good problem-solvers using a flexible repertoire of strategies.

Teachers also need to understand how students learn. What developmental issues must be addressed? How do students learn cooperatively in groups? How does the mathematics curriculum fit into the total educational picture for students at any one time? Only then can teachers determine worthwhile mathematical tasks for their students.

With the investigative approach to mathematics, teachers must follow good practices in discourse with students. What questions trigger the next step? What instructional strategies work with each student? What depth of mathematical thinking is effective now? At all times, teachers must listen critically to their students, both when they converse with them directly and when students discuss mathematics among themselves. In this way, teachers can monitor student achievement and help students self-monitor their progress.

Because learning should be both active and interactive, teachers need to comfortably use a variety of mathematical tools. Beyond mathematical symbols lies the standard selection of pictures, diagrams, and graphs. What models would be useful to clarify a math concept? What manipulatives help concretize an abstraction? Would a book or story illuminate a mathematical puzzle? Of course, technology offers a vast array of options: different types of calculators, subject-specific and open-ended computer software, Internet sources, videotapes and recording equipment to document and analyze mathematical phenomenon, measurement tools such as stopwatches and pressure gauges, presentation technology, and many others. Moreover, new technologies extend current skills and make possible new skills, such as zooming in/out, stop-motion analysis, and varying sequencing. Each tool has its advantages and disadvantages, and teachers need to determine which set is the most effective for each mathematical activity.

Finally, teachers need to analyze their own teaching. How well did students learn? What worked in the activity and what didn't? Why? One factor in a lesson can significantly affect student outcomes. How is each student learning? What challenges will extend their knowledge, or what accommodations will help them succeed? Constant assessment is needed to improve instructional planning and implementation.

THE ROLE OF INFORMATION LITERACY

Incorporating information literacy may seem like an unnecessary complication in the mathematical picture, yet those skills meld seamlessly with mathematical thinking. Particularly as students seek data from the real world, they need to know how to locate and evaluate those sources. After all, conclusions are only as good as the information upon which they are based.

The American Library Association applies three standards to information literacy: accessing information efficiently and effectively, evaluating information critically and competently, and using information effectively and creatively. Sounds like a generalized version of mathematical literacy, doesn't it? The American Association of School Librarians offers a list of problem-solving skills as a subset of information literacy:

- Defining the need for information; framing the need and relating information to prior knowledge
- Initiating the search strategy: organizing ideas, selecting key terms, identifying multiple sources
- Locating resources: accessing sources and specific information
- Assessing and comprehending the information: identifying and assessing relevant information, comparing sources
- Interpreting the information: using the sources to solve the information problem
- Communicating the information: determining the purpose for communication and developing the product
- Evaluating the product and process: how could it be done better?

As with current mathematical education, information literacy emphasizes process rather than "the right answer," and centers on the learner rather than the educator. It encourages connections within and across knowledge bases. It also acknowledges the ever-increasing spectrum of information and information sources: databases to Internet, artifacts to people, video to DVD.

Indeed, technology plays a significant role in information literacy, just as it does in mathematical exploration. Software programs such as Mathematica correspond to electronic databases in their ability to manipulate information. Hardware such as programmable graphing calculators can work in tandem with computer workstations to extract and display information. For both mathematical and information literacy, technology offers several advantages for students:

- access to more data
- more ways to interact with the data
- more opportunities to work with others
- more options for communicating findings

One possible drawback to the conscious incorporation of information literacy and accessing resources outside the textbook is the teacher's need to know these skills so that effective coaching can occur. What if the teacher does not feel confident in this area? How much extra time will this added skill take—and possibly detract from mathematical thinking? However, just as students should practice working cooperatively in order to maximize learning, so educators too need to collaborate to provide high-quality learning experiences. Library media teachers are the perfect partner in this endeavor. They have a broad-based perspective about information: sources, access tools, research strategies, selection and evaluation criteria. By consulting the library media teacher during the lesson-planning stage, the math teacher can find out the accessibility of certain data and, thus, shape the lesson to maximize the students' success rate. Knowing that data can be found in different forms, the math teacher can confidently have the students form heterogeneous working teams to compare data sources, for instance. The library media teacher can also suggest alternative data sources or acquire needed resources so a lesson will be more effective. If students conduct their math research in the library media center or lab, the library media teacher can serve as an instructional leader and coach to help students hone both math and information skills.

TEACHING MATH USING SPORTS TRAINING TECHNIQUES

This book uses sports as the context for math exploration and as a means to engage students through their natural interest in this subject. Because sports has so many aspects, a broad range of mathematical strands can be addressed from this perspective. Usually the teacher can start with the students' own experiences and then challenge them to think mathematically about the sport. Especially if the teacher points out that such thinking will likely improve student sports performance and appreciation of the game, students will "buy into" the learning experience.

Indeed, the teacher acts as a training coach in this series of mathematical units. Just as kids tire of free play and want a coach to help them excel, so teachers can ensure good math habits and give pointers for excellence. To this end, sports training principles work well in the math arena:

1. Aim for total conditioning: strength, flexibility, endurance, healthy mind.
2. Balance the choice of activity to include all types of mathematics.
3. Balance the choice of activity to address different aspects of each math strand.
4. Start with a needs analysis of each student.
5. Set reasonable goals.
6. Consider what kind of mathematical "energy" is needed for each activity, such as rapid response, detail work, persistent trial and error.
7. Consider what tools may help the training, such as manipulatives, calculators, etc.

8. Pace the session: start with warm-ups, do a workout, cool down with "stretchers" or reflections. (Note: warm-up exercises should point to the main purpose of the activity; warm-ups help students gear up to the main activity and adjust to a more demanding pace.)

9. Train in moderate doses with reflection/process time in between.

10. Overload: activities should challenge students a little so they will grow.

11. Use it or lose it: make sure students have opportunities to practice math skills.

12. To develop mathematical speed, do quick-response exercises.

13. To develop mathematical flexibility, use a variety of problems that have a variety of answers.

14. To develop mathematical endurance, use easier problems and lots of them.

15. To develop mathematical power, use harder problems (more mental resistance) with fewer "repeats."

16. Ensure proper progression: from simple to complex, from short periods to extended ones, from easy to challenging, with proper demonstration before starting.

17. Prevent mathematical "injuries" or failures by setting a safe "course" and practices; take care of injuries quickly so the student can get back up to speed.

18. If a problem "hurts," stop.

19. Check the "pulse rate" during math "workouts."

20. Evaluate performance and adjust training accordingly; encourage students to compete against themselves.

21. Think of the class as a league, and small cooperative groups as teams; this encourages both cooperative team work and healthy competition.

Now, let the (math) games begin!

Framework for Math Units

This book provides units that explore mathematical concepts using a meaningful sports context. Five major topics are covered, each with its own mathematical focus. For each topic, units proceed from single-concept exercises (usually termed "warm-up") to extensive open-ended projects (called "marathon"). Likewise, the material usually proceeds from the simplest mathematical concepts to the most complex. Subdivisions then focus on individual sports.

The physiology unit, "Body Works," focuses on measurement. Beginning with each person's body measurements, students compare data within the class, the school and community, and beyond. Next, mathematical models of physical systems such as circulation and respiration help students learn how their bodies work. Students hypothesize about factors that correlate with significant physiological data differences, such as gender, age, and the environment.

The training unit, "Be All That You Can Be," focuses on functions. Students explore math concepts that relate to overall physical fitness and sport-specific training. They also deal with independent–dependent variables that affect sports improvement, and compare their progress with the status of model athletes.

"Knowing the Ropes," with an emphasis on geometry, is the third unit. It covers math related to rules and the physics of sports. By examining mathematical principles behind sports, students can improve their playing techniques.

The sports competition unit, "Playing the Odds," focuses on statistics. Students examine the varied statistics within and between each sport, and draw conclusions about individual and team performance. They also test hypotheses about factors that influence performance (e.g., age, environment, physical condition) and ascertain trends over time.

The last unit, "Sports for (Fun and) Profit," examines economics, emphasizing data representation (e.g., graphs and spreadsheets). Students explore the income and expenditures for amateur and professional sports from several perspectives. As a final activity, students explore sports-related careers for themselves.

These different types of activities challenge students in different ways. "Warm-ups" help students focus, and are intended to call upon their prior math knowledge. These exercises are a good way to start a class session, and can usually be done independently. "Workouts" comprise the main body of the activity; they offer opportunities for substantive mathematical investigation and allow the student some say in shaping their experience. "Stretchers" challenge students to make connections to other topics or other ways of thinking, thus stretching their imaginations so they will become more flexible mathematical thinkers. "Marathons" are open-ended activities that synthesize a variety of math activities; they are intended to be done in small cooperative teams, and may be used to assess complex learning with real-life authenticity. "Dugouts" are fun sports or math facts or questions that provide a break, and may stimulate students to pursue that topic in more depth. Each activity can be approached at different levels of math sophistication, just as many physical activities can be done by beginners, regulars, and professionals. The teacher and student together can determine which level is appropriate.

16 Framework for Math Units

WORKOUT/MARATHON TEMPLATE

The following is a key to the structures of all the major activities in the book. Be aware that there are many cross-mathematical and cross-sport ideas and possible adaptations for the units presented.

- ☑ **ACTIVITY DESCRIPTION:** A one-sentence general description of the math activity.

- ☑ **SPORTS:** A list of sports addressed in the activity.

- ☑ **MATHEMATICAL STRAND OUTCOMES:** A list of student performances, products, or knowledge related to a mathematical topic.

- ☑ **INFORMATION LITERACY OUTCOMES:** A list of student performances, products, or knowledge related to the processing of data. Most activities combine these skills: locating and selecting data sources, critically evaluating them, organizing and synthesizing data, and sharing results.

- ☑ **PREREQUISITE SKILLS:** A list of those skills or concepts that students should exhibit prior to beginning the activity. For example, if students are supposed to convert measurements, then they should be able to use conversion formulas. An activity may be used without the prerequisite skills, but the skills must be introduced and practiced before the activity can be accomplished.

- ☑ **RATIONALE FOR THE ACTIVITY:** This section answers the pedagogical question, "Why are we doing this?" The issues and problems raised in this section are explored through the related activity. Student outcomes should be shared with students at the beginning of major explorations.

- ☑ **COACHING TIPS:** This section guides the classroom and librarian teachers as they facilitate student learning. Helping hints and ideas for modifying the activity are included.

WARM-UPS

- ☑ **DESCRIPTION:** Brief mathematical exercises that set the stage for ensuing mathematical concepts and help students focus on the task at hand.

STUDENT GAME PLAN

- ☑ **CONTEXT:** This section is the motivational, contextual "hook." It provides background sports information leading to the math problem.

- ☑ **CHALLENGE:** This section specifies the math problem. Enough guidance is provided to structure the activity yet offer options for students to shape their experience.

- ☑ **TASKS:** The specific steps that students carry out independently. The warm-up is usually done before the game plan is introduced, but it can be used as a "pre" step to focus students.

- ☑ **RESOURCES:** A general list of the types of resources that students use to accomplish the task.

- ☑ **ASSESSMENT:** Each activity is evaluated on several levels: understanding, process, evidence, and communication. Both individual and teamwork should be assessed. Students may take individual format tests or document their individual learning.

- ☑ **STRETCHERS:** Other activities are included to provide students with another perspective or added factor to the problem.

- ☑ **DUGOUT:** These interesting questions or facts act as brainteasers and brain relaxers.

Part II
Body Works

How Do You Measure Up?

TEACHER PLAY BOOK

- ☑ **ACTIVITY DESCRIPTION:** Students measure their own bodies and compare them with standard units of length.

- ☑ **SPORTS:** Physiology

- ☑ **MATHEMATICAL STRAND OUTCOMES:** Students will:
  - calculate personal measurements in relation to standard units
  - calculate body measurements using proportions
  - explain the origins of "standard" measures
  - convert measurements from one system to another

- ☑ **INFORMATION LITERACY OUTCOMES:** Students will:
  - locate information about different measurement systems

- ☑ **PREREQUISITE SKILLS:**
  - understanding the concept of proportion
  - awareness of measurement systems

- ☑ **RATIONALE FOR THE ACTIVITY:** Let's start at the beginning: the personal. Middle schoolers, in particular, have a fascination with their bodies. They are experiencing growth and change, and often don't understand it. Their social needs almost *dictate* that they compare their bodies. This period in development also marks the greatest apparent discrepancy between males and females as girls start maturing earlier. This activity provides a rational way to explore these differences and to accept them all.

- ☑ **COACHING TIPS:** Because body measurements can be a sensitive subject for students, care is needed in introducing this activity. Students need to be reminded about confidentiality and the idea of measuring against oneself rather than against others. Giving the topic a historical perspective helps diffuse the giggles. Pair students by same sex as they measure themselves; one option is to let students write down the names of a couple of people they would feel comfortable being measured by so that the teacher can assign pairs the next day. Try having one half of the class use a metric tape measure, and the other half use an English tape.

WARM-UPS

1. The earliest known standard unit of measurement is the *cubit*, which was used by the Egyptians 5,000 years ago. It was based on the length of a man's hand and forearm. Ancient documents mention the cubit; the Bible states that the giant Goliath was exactly 6 cubits and a *span* (1 Samuel 17:4). Given that a span is half a cubit, measure your teacher's cubit length. Use that measurement to calculate Goliath's height.

   a. The original definition of a span was the length of an extended hand: from the tip of the little finger to the tip of the thumb. Again, measuring your teacher, does that proportion reflect the relationship between a cubit and a span?

   b. Over time, people's bodies have increased in size. What height do you think Goliath really was? Do you think the relationship between a span and a cubit has changed over time? When people's bodies grow, do they keep the same proportions?

2. Horse height is traditionally measured in *hands*, the width of a closed hand from the outside thumb edge to the outside palm edge. The height of a horse is measured from the ground to the top of the shoulder blades (the *wither*). Using your teacher's measurement, how high is a horse of 18 hands? (Draft horses are often that size.)

   a. The standard length of a hand is 4 inches or 10 centimeters. Recalculate the horse's height. What is the proportional difference?

   b. Ponies are defined as less than 14 hands, 2 inches tall. What is the measurement in feet? In meters?

STUDENT GAME PLAN

☑ **CONTEXT:** King John of England really put his foot in it that time in England. But it was his choice. He declared that the main measure of length would be the *foot*, and that the legal length was the length of *his* foot. That length is still used today, as the foot became the basis for the English measurement system called the imperial system. Other measurement systems also used the body as the basis for units, and are still useful when estimating lengths. Even today, tailors will often measure fabric by holding one end up to their nose (with their head away from their outstretched arm) and pulling the cloth to the tips of their fingers to designate a yard. Watch that phenomenon in the fabric store sometime.

☑ **CHALLENGE:** Be the center of the measurement universe! Devise your own measurement system based on your body measurements. Use it to measure items. Then convert your system to the English system and the metric (known in scientific circles as the Système International).

☑ **TASKS:**

1. Determine which body measurements to use. You may want to research what other measurement terms have been derived from the body, such as *stride* or *digit*.

2. After you make your measurements, see what relationships exist between body parts. Make equations to show these relationships.

3. Develop an original measurement system based on your measurements. One measurement unit will probably be the main one (like the foot or the meter).

4. Choose different things to measure, and determine the size in terms of your system. You might try measuring a room. (How would you do that?)

5. With a partner (probably the one who helped measure you), convert things from your measurement system to theirs. Use their system to measure things. Compare the two systems. Are there similarities or interesting relationships between the two systems?

☑ **RESOURCES:** Tape measures; sources of information on the history of measurement systems; measurement conversion tables.

☑ **ASSESSMENT:** Your final project should consist of a table of your measurement system and documentation showing items measured and converted. You will be assessed in terms of your accuracy, process, and final reflections.

☑ **STRETCHERS:**

1. Though the metric system is used in science, what other measurement systems have been used in the past or in other cultures? How were they derived? How do they relate to the English system or the Système International (SI)?

2. What is the meaning of the measurement unit *foot candle?* Can you think of other measurement units based on body parts?

3. People sometimes measure a room by *pacing* it. What does that mean? How accurate do you think it is? How consistent (reliable) would it be? Why?

DUGOUT

"I can't fathom Mark Twain." How would you say that in measurement terms?

"I can't 6-feet a measurement of 12 feet [2 fathoms]."

Where's the Perfect Body?

TEACHER PLAY BOOK

☑ **ACTIVITY DESCRIPTION:** Students develop surveys about body measurements and derive statistical information from them. They then compare their results with other measurement tables.

☑ **SPORTS:** Physiology, all

☑ **MATHEMATICAL STRAND OUTCOMES:** Students will:
- plan and implement a survey about body measurements
- generate statistical information based on the survey
- differentiate between samples and populations
- develop hypotheses and draw conclusions based on the survey and statistics

☑ **INFORMATION LITERACY OUTCOMES:** Students will:
- access sources having measurement tables
- access sources about body measurements or "ideal" bodies
- analyze measurement tables

☑ **PREREQUISITE SKILLS:**
- basic understanding of surveys
- basic understanding of statistical information

☑ **RATIONALE FOR THE ACTIVITY:** People often compare their bodies with others. The media pushes certain body types as ideal, even if they might not be healthy. Interestingly, in different periods in history, different body proportions have been touted as desirable. This activity lets students explore the statistical differences in body measurements and make predictions about body measurements based on their analysis. Students may also investigate body changes over time.

☑ **COACHING TIPS:** As in the "How Do You Measure Up?" activity, care must be taken to keep measurements confidential. Let the students figure out a way to make a survey with confidentiality in mind. If the class has done the "Measure Up" activity, the first survey can be generated as a class warm-up. Students can then brainstorm other measurements, such as height, weight, shoe size, head circumference, and waist size. They should also brainstorm ways to divide the class into two (or more) subpopulations that may be significantly different: by gender, by birthday, by recreational activity, etc. If students survey other groups, remind them to get proper permission. Also remind students to give the proper citation information about other measurement tables or information they use. This activity is best done in small, heterogeneous, cooperative teams; allow students enough time to decide how to distribute the tasks. This activity may be done at different levels of mathematical sophistication: an easy extension is to teach students how to use a chi-square statistic to test for significant differences; inferences about population distributions may be pursued by older students.

WARM-UPS

1. Recent studies indicate that two-thirds of Americans are overweight. How can that be if the average weight should be at the 50% mark?

2. Barbie has been considered the ideal female figure in the late 20th century. Do you agree? Her original measurements were 11.5 inches high, 6.6-inch bust, 3.13-inch waist, 5.9-inch hips; her 1998 measurements are supposed to reflect a more realistic female. If she were your height, what would her proportionate measurements be? Do you think you'd have an ideal body if it looked like hers? Why did her measurements change? Research the answer. Do you think they should have? Why?

STUDENT GAME PLAN

☑ **CONTEXT:** You look at the advertisements, and those models don't have your body. Who's closer to normal or to perfect? Even in your class, what's average? How different are bodies anyway? Maybe models are aliens — or at least another population from "regular" people. What do you think are ideal body measurements?

☑ **CHALLENGE:** Do a reality check on body measurements by getting the facts. Starting with your class, develop a survey to determine statistically the variations and similarities of body measurements. As part of your survey, hypothesize whether a specific correlation exists between two measurements. For instance, some say that the length of the forearm is the same as the foot size. Is that true? To check the reliability of your hypothesis, survey another group of people or consult an existing body measurement chart.

☑ **TASKS:**

1. Form one hypothesis about differences in body measurements or proportions of two groups within your class; for instance, do students who participate in sports have a significantly different height-to-weight ratio from students who do not?

2. Form a second hypothesis about body measurements and proportional correlations (ratios) in your class.

3. Develop survey questions that would get at the information you need to test your hypotheses.

4. Plan and conduct the survey. Think about who you will survey (consider sampling techniques), how you will get the information, and how you will organize the information.

5. Generate statistics that give an accurate picture of your class and would confirm or negate your hypotheses. Remember that it's OK if your hypothesis is null (not proved); the important thing is to calculate and use statistical information accurately.

6. Plan and conduct a survey of another group of people to test the reliability of your hypothesis. You may want to predict a different outcome by surveying a group you think would be significantly different (by age, geographic location, occupation, period in history). As an option, you may consult existing body measurement charts.

7. Generate and analyze the statistical evidence to make conclusions about your hypothesis. Also address the issue of populations; do your two samples belong to the same population or not? Why?

☑ **RESOURCES:** Measurement tools, calculators to derive statistics (optional); spreadsheet computer program to generate table (optional); outside sources of body measurement tables (e.g., fitness books).

☑ **ASSESSMENT:** Your final project will consist of tables of your surveys, your hypotheses, a list of survey questions, your method of surveying people, statistics from your surveys and analysis of those statistics, and conclusions about your project. Also answer the question "Where's the perfect body?" You will be assessed on the accuracy and thoroughness of your procedures, findings, and analysis.

☑ **STRETCHERS:**

1. Traditional drawing instruction divides the human body into eight sections, with the head being one section long. Sectioning off the body parts, keeping each one proportional, makes it easier for the artist to draw different sizes and different perspectives. There are also ideal proportions at various ages. The classic book on this approach is Loomis's *Figure Drawing* (1946), although Leonardo da Vinci was probably the most famous Renaissance artist to use this approach in drawing the body. Find drawing guides and apply them to your survey figures. As a related activity, assume that people, regardless of age, are the same size. Draw their proportionate differences based on that assumption.

2. It's hard to be an all-around athlete. Imagine a linebacker as a jockey — or a gymnast as a shot putter. Find the average body measurements of professional athletes, and compare them between sports. Predict the implications of their performance — and the game's outcome.

3. Society's concept of the ideal body has changed over the ages, and differs among cultures. Research those differences and create a table of the findings. Generate statistical information about the measurements and draw conclusions about them.

DUGOUT

Who has more muscles? Arnold Schwarzenegger or Twiggy?

They have the same number of muscles: about 600.

Let Me Measure the Ways

TEACHER PLAY BOOK

☑ **ACTIVITY DESCRIPTION:** Students take a variety of measurements related to the body, and discover mathematical relationships among them.

☑ **SPORTS:** Physiology, all

☑ **MATHEMATICAL STRAND OUTCOMES:** Students will:
- measure different aspects of the body
- define and use a variety of measurement systems
- convert measurements
- create a scatterplot
- make predictions and draw conclusions based on data

☑ **INFORMATION LITERACY OUTCOMES:** Students will:
- locate and use weights and measures tables
- organize data for analysis and presentation

☑ **PREREQUISITE SKILLS:**
- basic skills in measurement
- ability to use measurement tools (optional)

☑ **RATIONALE FOR THE ACTIVITY:** Students often do not realize the number of "flavors" that measurements come in. Nor do they realize how different measurements are interrelated. Using the body as the focus, students have an opportunity to explore these concepts. Students also become more aware of ways to measure the inside of the body, both directly and indirectly.

☑ **COACHING TIPS:** Help students brainstorm different measurements that describe the body. As much as possible, let students research ways to measure the body and find appropriate measuring tools. If possible, incorporate the use of scientific probes and other computer/calculator peripherals to help students quantify and graph the data. Have students do a walkabout to read about the different measurements posted; they may then take the summary sheet to help them with the second part of the activity. This half of the project works well with pairs: one to measure and one to record. Remind students that a mathematical correlation requires that one compare measurement units; they would do well to use the metric system. Students may need to review how to generate a scatterplot to determine possible correlations. Students may need help in drafting an experimental report; you may provide them with an example for them to critique, and then have them look for an existing study in a science magazine to follow.

WARM-UPS

1. Joe Montana is 6 feet, 2 inches tall and weighs 195 pounds. Shaquille O'Neal is 7 feet, 1 inch tall and weighs 303 pounds. How tall would Montana have to be (at his present weight) in order to be as dense as O'Neal?

    a. At his present height, how much weight would Montana have to gain to be as dense as O'Neal?

    b. What percentage of his present weight would that constitute?

2. One scientific indicator of healthy weight is the Body Mass Index (BMI). Its formula is: weight in pounds multiplied by 700), divided by the square of height in inches. A BMI of 25 or less indicates very low to low risk for heart disease and high blood pressure. If a person is 5 feet, 2 inches, what would their weight be in order to have a 25 BMI? If you convert weight to kilograms and height to centimeters, what would the multiplying factor (now 700) have to be instead?

3. If an astronaut is weightless, does he or she have zero mass? Why?

STUDENT GAME PLAN

☑ **CONTEXT:** To diagnose a patient's relative health, doctors measure the human body in several ways: stethoscope for heart rate, sphygmomanometer for blood pressure, thermometer for temperature, and so on. Sports trainers also measure the body to determine physical fitness: running speed, endurance, fat content. Measurements — and bodies — really do exist in many forms, each with its own value.

☑ **CHALLENGE:** How many ways can you measure the body in order to determine physical fitness? In addition to linear measure for height, there are basic measurements of time, temperature, mass, rotation, and derivative measurements such as density (volume/area). Investigate these different measurements and what they can tell you about the human body. See if there are correlations between measurements and their implications for fitness or sports.

☑ **TASKS:**

1. Identify possible indicators for physical fitness and the ways to measure those indicators. For instance, a simple measure of physical ability is the height of a standing jump. Called the *Sargent jump* (named after an early physical education leader), it measures the distance between the height reached by the upward extended hand of a person standing straight against a wall and the height of the hand at the highest point of the standing jump. The average college student's jump is 20 inches.

2. Research ways to measure the body using at least two different types of measurements (e.g., temperature and mass) and locate the relevant measurement tools. One of the measurements should be a derivative, such as volume. Look for alternative ways to measure factors in order to find the most reasonable method. For instance, an easy way to measure reaction time is to use a ruler. Hold a ruler vertically just above a second person's fingers (thumb and forefinger together). Without warning, drop the ruler. Measure the distance it takes for the person to catch the ruler between those two fingers.

3. Create a one-page summary for each measurement including the following information: a definition, what it measures, its implications for fitness, method(s) of measurement. Post all the summaries for the class to see.

4. With another person, choose two measurements from the posted options that may be correlated, such as lung capacity and weight. Form a hypothesis about the correlation, and research information about a possible correlation.

5. Develop a plan to test the correlation experimentally.

6. Implement the plan, gathering data. To organize the data, create a scatterplot, with one axis representing one measure and the other axis representing the other.

7. Determine what correlation, if any, exists between the two sets of data. Remember, it's OK if no correlation exists (although mildly disappointing) so long as the figures are accurate.

☑ **RESOURCES:** Sources of information on measurement and measurement tools; calculators to derive statistics (optional); spreadsheet computer program to generate table (optional); outside sources of body measurement tables (such as fitness books).

☑ **ASSESSMENT:** Your project should consist of three parts: the one-sheet measurement summaries, the scatterplot, and the plan. You will be assessed in terms of your accuracy and thoroughness, your plan, and your final conclusions.

☑ **STRETCHERS:**

1. Examine studies about body measurements and base your plan on an existing research effort. This method is used by most scientists and researchers.

2. Are fairy tale giants feasible? Assuming a person were three times your height and body proportions were maintained, what would be the circumference of the person's knee? However, bone strength depends on the cross-sectional area of bones while body weight depends on the cubic relationship (volume). So how heavy would the person be? What would happen to their legs? Read sections from *The World of Mathematics* (Newman, 1956) and *The Realm of Measure* (Asimov, 1960) to find out more.

3. The male broad jump record is 8.95 meters; the women's record is 7.52 meters. An impala can jump 30 to 40 feet, a rabbit can jump 25 feet, and a cricket frog can jump 3 feet. What inferences can you make about this data?

DUGOUT

If your big toe is longer than your second toe, you have a natural advantage in skiing and sprinting. Why?

It's easier to lean onto it, and it can exert twice as much force as your second toe. What a feat!

Composing a Body

TEACHER PLAY BOOK

☑ **ACTIVITY DESCRIPTION:** Students take indirect measurements related to body composition.

☑ **SPORTS:** Physiology, all

☑ **MATHEMATICAL STRAND OUTCOMES:** Students will:
- make indirect measurements
- draw inferences from indirect data
- calculate data on body composition
- organize raw data into graph/chart form
- determine which kind of graph/chart best represents different types of data

☑ **INFORMATION LITERACY OUTCOMES:** Students will:
- locate and use information about body composition
- make reasonable inferences from information
- interpret graphical information

☑ **PREREQUISITE SKILLS:**
- ability to draw a graph and a chart

☑ **RATIONALE FOR THE ACTIVITY:** Sometimes it is difficult to take direct measurements. However, indirect measurements can lead one to make reasonable inferences about hard-to-measure situations. Additionally, raw measurements may be difficult to interpret; by organizing data into visual graphs and charts, students can draw conclusions more readily. This activity uses body composition to concretize these mathematical concepts.

☑ **COACHING TIPS:** This activity is divided into two parts. First, students research the body's composition; then they apply their finding to a particular sport. Because there are four major components, the class should be divided into four cooperative teams, with each person researching one aspect of the topic. For the second part of the activity, create new teams of four members each, one from each of the original teams. You may need to review the different types of graphs and charts, and how each one represents different kinds of data.

WARM-UPS

1. If you separate blood into its components (by spinning it in a centrifuge), you will find that about half of it is plasma (pale yellow fluid). Plasma itself is about 90% water. The last 10% is sugar, nutrients, acids, salts, minerals, and proteins (Parker 1994, 103). About 45% of the blood consists of red blood cells. A little less than 1% of blood consists of white blood cells and platelets. If there are 250,000 platelets for every 10,000 white blood cells, what would be the weight of the white cells in a gallon of blood? In a gallon of plasma substances (non-water), what would be the weight of the platelets?

2. A typical adult male's body is 15% fat; a female's is 27%. Of that percentage, 78% of the male's fat is storage fat, while 51% of the female's is storage fat. If the average weight of a man is 57 kilograms, and the average for a woman is 47 kilograms, what is the weight of the storage fat of each?

   a. Of the male's fat, 22% is essential fat; for the female it is 27%. What are the relative weights of each?

   b. In addition, 22% of the female's fat is sex-specific. What would be the proportional weight based on the above figures?

 # STUDENT GAME PLAN

☑ **CONTEXT:** "What are little boys made of?" 45% muscle, 15% bone, 15% fat, 25% other for a typical adult male of 175 centimeters (5 feet, 9 inches) and 57 kilograms (154 lbs). "What are little girls made of?" 36% muscle, 12% bone, 27% fat, 25% other for a typical adult female 163 centimeters (5 feet, 4 inches) and 47 kilograms (125 lbs) (Zumerchik, 1997, 617).

☑ **CHALLENGE:** The greater the body's fat content percentage, the more easily and the longer a person will float. Women have been known to swim longer distances with less energy strain than men. Why? In what other sports might the reduction or increase in the relative proportion of body composition influence performance? Create the ideal body composition for a specific sport.

☑ **TASKS:**

1. Choose one component of body composition: muscle, fat, bone, or other.

2. Find out what measurements are used in conjunction with that component and for what purpose.

3. Within your team, take some measurements related to your topic and generate graphs or charts to represent the data. Draw conclusions based on your findings.

4. In a new team (composed of one representative from each component), choose a sport and research the body demands for optimum performance in that sport.

5. Generate a pie chart showing the relative percentages of each body component that would be ideal for your sport.

☑ **RESOURCES:** Sources of information on sports and body composition; graphing tools.

☑ **ASSESSMENT:** Your final project should consist of a pie chart and a rationale for your conclusions. You will be assessed on the appearance and accuracy of your chart, your supporting documentation, and the process by which you arrived at your conclusions.

☑ STRETCHERS:

1. At different ages, the body needs to adjust the relative percentages of body components. Research the differences in relative percentages over time and by gender. Create comparative graphs. Determine the reasons for these changes.

2. One major factor in energy expenditure is metabolism: the rate that a body burns fuel. Women have about a 5 to 10% lower metabolism than men. How does body composition affect this rate? How does metabolism affect sports performance?

DUGOUT

The heaviest Olympic wrestler was Chris Taylor, at 420 pounds.

Emergency Systems

TEACHER PLAY BOOK

☑ **ACTIVITY DESCRIPTION:** Students measure different body systems and draw inferences about their interaction.

☑ **SPORTS:** Physiology

☑ **MATHEMATICAL STRAND OUTCOMES:** Students will:
- identify mathematical concepts, particularly measurements, related to different body systems
- determine normal ranges and exceptional figures for body measurement
- identify and distinguish between dependent and independent variables

☑ **INFORMATION LITERACY OUTCOMES:**
- locate information about different body systems and their measurements
- make predictions based on data
- organize data into database format

☑ **PREREQUISITE SKILLS:**
- generating and calculating ratios and percentages
- basic statistical skills
- database manipulation
- collaborative work

☑ **RATIONALE FOR THE ACTIVITY:** The body operates based on the functioning and interaction of a variety of systems. Each one manifests its own set of mathematical measurements and concepts. This activity helps students understand how measurement can explain bodily functions and assists in making predictions about them, particularly in relation to other body systems.

☑ **COACHING TIPS:** Have students brainstorm the body's systems. The list should include musculoskeletal (covered in the "Composing a Body" activity), respiratory, digestive, circulatory, nervous, reproductive, urinary, lymphatic, endocrine, and immune. Group students by system; one may do the research and the other create the data entries. Ideally, the class should develop the database fields, which should include system name, measurement, normal range (per gender), and effects on the system (and other systems) if measurement is outside the norm. It is easiest to dedicate one workstation to the class database input; however, students will have to manage their time wisely to avoid long wait times. Another option, if computers are networked, is to place the class database on a "commons" folder so a number of people can access it simultaneously. This arrangement also facilitates the diagnostic process. If computers are not networked, copies of the database file may be made on diskettes and then imported onto other machines. If there are no computers, then students can create a paper database, with one card per record. For ease of access the card sets should be posted in some order (which the class can determine). Be sure to assess the database before starting the next step; corrections need to be made so students will not misdiagnose their patients. Encourage students to consult other resources after they have worked with the class database in conjunction with their patient data.

WARM-UPS

1. The average adult body contains 5,500 milliliters of blood: 2,750 milliliters in the veins, 1,100 milliliters in the lungs, 825 milliliters in the arteries, 550 milliliters in the heart, and 275 milliliters in the capillaries (Ricci 1967, 202). What is this distribution in percentages? Generate a pie chart representing these figures.

2. When people are cold, they often curl up or start shivering. What is the effect of these actions? Why do they work?

    a. The body loses heat roughly in these proportions: 42% radiation, 26% convection, 18% sweat evaporation, and 14% breathing. Create a pie chart of this distribution.

    b. A sweat loss of more than 7% of your body weight can lead to circulatory problems and possibly death. How much water loss is that for your body?

- ☑ **CONTEXT:** The body is like a complex city, full of different systems that function both separately and interconnectively. Just as a traffic jam affects business and safety, so does a heart attack affect respiratory and nervous systems as well as the circulatory system.

- ☑ **CHALLENGE:** You're the doctor in a hospital emergency room. Help! An adult comes in and you must diagnose what's wrong and possible consequences based on the measurements of the body system.

- ☑ **TASKS:**

    1. Choose one body system. Find out what measurements apply to that system.

    2. Research the normal measurements for an average adult male and female. Find out the effects of a change from the normal range, both to that system and possibly to other systems.

    3. Create a database record for each measurement and input it into the class database.

    4. Create three cards (2.5 by 3 inches is a good size) for each measurement: one normal, one high, and one low. For instance, this could be 94°F, 98.6°F, and 103°F for body temperature (don't include unreasonable figures such as 120°F).

    5. From the class card set of measurements, pick three cards at random. If more than one applies to the same measurement, pick another card.

    6. Based on the chosen cards, diagnose the patient's problem(s) and predict what will happen next. You may get conflicting data, such as a high temperature and a slow heart rate. If so, state the discrepancy, pose a possible reason for the discrepancy, and decide how to handle the data. Consider consulting other resources after using the class database information.

- ☑ **RESOURCES:** Sources of information on body systems, measurement, and medical diagnoses; database software; card stock (half-sized index cards).

- ☑ **ASSESSMENT:** Your final project should consist of two parts: your database entries and your diagnosis. You will be assessed on the accuracy and thoroughness of your entries and your diagnosis. Equally important will be the process by which you made your diagnosis and predictions.

☑ **STRETCHERS:**

1. Choose another age for the patient and derive the appropriate measurements and diagnoses.

2. Research logical treatments for the patient, based on the measurements and diagnosis.

3. Start with a medical problem, such as a stroke or a stomach bullet wound, and predict the likely measurements for the body's different systems.

DUGOUT

If you lined up all the blood vessels in a body end to end, how long would the line be?

100,000 kilometers.

Marathon: Body Morph

TEACHER PLAY BOOK

☑ **ACTIVITY DESCRIPTION:** Students create a hypermedia decision game that tests the effects of changes in body measurements.

☑ **SPORTS:** Physiology

☑ **MATHEMATICAL STRAND OUTCOMES:** Students will:
- calculate conversions accurately
- determine appropriate measurements
- develop decision trees
- determine correlations between data
- make accurate predictions based on data
- represent data in chart form

☑ **INFORMATION LITERACY OUTCOMES:**
- locate information about body systems and measurements
- determine main ideas
- organize and present data using an authoring program

☑ **PREREQUISITE SKILLS:**
- knowledge about measurement and body systems
- basic awareness of permutations

☑ **RATIONALE FOR THE ACTIVITY:** The body is a complex organism that is highly interdependent. So, too, are measurements related, particularly in the metric system. This marathon activity allows students to synthesize their knowledge about measurements and the body, as well as polish their hypothesis and decision-making skills. It also helps students visualize how only one change can have significant ramifications. This activity can form the basis of an introduction to chaos theory.

☑ **COACHING TIPS:** Have students brainstorm actions or decisions that would affect the body, such as smoking, falling, getting pregnant, taking up exercising, contracting a disease, or losing weight. Emphasize the need for careful research so students will make logical predictions and calculations. If there are no computers, students can make decision trees by hand.

STUDENT GAME PLAN

☑ **CONTEXT:** It's been said that the fluttering of a butterfly wing in Australia can affect the weather in the United States. In the film *Jurassic Park*, for instance, the mathematician explains how one small change in a system can totally transform it. On the personal level, you know how a cold can really undermine you academically and socially. It can get chaotic!

☑ **CHALLENGE:** "Morph" the human body. Demonstrate how changes in the body, as evidenced in measurement differences, affect the system.

☑ **TASKS:**

1. Choose a person. Determine his or her original characteristics and measurements.
2. Create an action that would lead to a change in body measurement, such as breaking a leg.
3. Predict and calculate the probable changes in body measurements.
4. Using the new data, determine how the body might change or adjust. In the case of a broken leg, a person would probably exercise less.
5. Based on body adjustments, predict and calculate the next changes in body measurements.
6. Once more, determine the body changes and subsequent measurement changes.
7. Create charts to show the mathematical changes in measurement. Derive statistical information about the changes.
8. Produce a hypermedia presentation with appropriate links to visualize these changes.

☑ **RESOURCES:** Sources of information on body systems and measurements; authoring software.

☑ **ASSESSMENT:** Your final project should consist of a hypermedia presentation incorporating the decision points, changes, and mathematical evidence. You will be assessed on the logic of your assumptions, the accuracy of your predictions and calculations, the thoroughness of your information, and the appearance of your presentation.

DUGOUT

The youngest major league baseball player was 14 years old: Fred Chapman, who pitched for Philadelphia. The oldest player was also a pitcher: The Kansas City Athletics' Satchel Paige at 59 years old.

Part III

Be All That You Can Be

You Are What You Eat

TEACHER PLAY BOOK

☑ **ACTIVITY DESCRIPTION:** Students develop nutritional plans.

☑ **SPORTS:** Physiology, training for all

☑ **MATHEMATICAL STRAND OUTCOMES:** Students will:
- explain and use data about calories
- calculate calories accurately
- calculate percentages accurately
- identify nutrition-related functions
- represent data in spreadsheet and pie chart form

☑ **INFORMATION LITERACY OUTCOMES:** Students will:
- locate information on nutrition
- read data in chart form

☑ **PREREQUISITE SKILLS:**
- ability to create a spreadsheet (optional)
- basic arithmetic skills

☑ **RATIONALE FOR THE ACTIVITY:** As young adults grow, their bodies have different nutritional needs. This activity helps students discover how calories are a function of nutrients.

☑ **COACHING TIPS:** To focus the topic, have students list their favorite (and least favorite) foods. Divide the list by gender preferences to help students in their subsequent nutrition plan. Students may need review in creating spreadsheets (especially in using formulas); if working in pairs, students may divide the work so that one researches and one inputs.

WARM-UPS

1. The recommended dietary allowance (RDA) of protein for adults is .8 grams per kilogram per day. How many grams of protein should a 150- or 120-pound woman consume daily?

    a. Another way to calculate the amount of protein is to derive it from the percentage of daily caloric intake. If an adult consumes 2,000 calories daily, and 12 to 15% of that should be protein, how many calories of protein should they eat?

    b. If 4 calories = 1 gram protein, how many grams of protein is the RDA for a man or woman?

    c. Your fat intake should be less than 10% of your total calories. If 9 calories = 1 gram fat, how many grams of fat does that make?

    d. What issues arise from your calculations?

2. If an adult were dehydrated, the remaining weight would be one-third of the original weight. How much would be your dry weight?

3. Here are some other water facts: the body needs to replenish its water supply to stay healthy. Even if you just sit around, you lose about 2 liters of water daily. If you exercise, you can lose 2 liters an hour. However, your stomach can process only 3 cups of water per hour. To measure water loss from exercise, weigh yourself just before you start and just after you stop (after drying yourself off). A pint of water equals 1 pound.

    a. How many pounds would you lose in two hours of hard exercise?

    b. How long will it take for your body to be replenished if you exercise hard for two hours? Justify your answer.

STUDENT GAME PLAN

☑ **CONTEXT:** It has been said, "You are what you eat." Ideally, that translates into the following: 2,300 calories for a 54-kilogram, 16-year-old girl or 3,000 calories for a 61-kilogram, 16-year-old boy (Goodhart 1980, 263). Calories are measurements of heat (specifically, the amount of energy needed to raise the temperature of 1 kilogram of water 1°C). But there's more than counting calories. These calories should comprise the following nutrient amounts:

	Girls	**Boys**
carbohydrates	346 g	450 g
fats	78 g	107 g
proteins	46 g	56 g

Vitamins and minerals also comprise part of your RDA (about 1% of the total calories). Then there's the food pyramid that you should follow. Maybe eating isn't as easy as you thought!

☑ **CHALLENGE:** You're the nutritionist for your school cafeteria, which has just been authorized to provide all of your meals. This service is paid for by tobacco taxes, so you don't have to shell out any money. (In most states you can't buy tobacco until you're 18 years old, and smoking isn't healthy anyway.) So what would be a healthy day's meal plan?

☑ **TASKS:**

1. Write down what you ate yesterday.
2. Find out the nutrient amounts for that food, and calculate the grams and percentages accordingly.
3. Represent the data in pie chart and spreadsheet format.
4. Create a nutritionally ideal and appealing menu for the day. (Forget three meals of grilled leeks and anchovies.) Because girls have slightly different needs, provide modifications to accommodate both genders (keeping them happy as well as healthy).
5. Find out the nutrient amounts for the food, and calculate the grams and percentages accordingly.
6. Represent the data in a separate pie chart, and incorporate it into the existing spreadsheet.

7. Using the spreadsheet program, calculate the gram and percentage differences between the two gender menus, and the difference between the ideal and the original meal (using the figures for your gender). (Note: if you're a boy 11 to 14 years old, adjust the caloric total to 2,800, maintaining the same nutritional percentages.)

8. Draw conclusions about the data and the process.

☑ **RESOURCES:** Sources of information on body nutritional requirements and food composition.

☑ **ASSESSMENT:** Your final project should consist of two series of data—your original daily intake and an ideal menu plan—in list, chart, and spreadsheet formats (include gender modifications), and activity reflections. You will be assessed on your mathematical accuracy, the healthiness and appeal of the plan, and the soundness of your process and conclusions.

☑ **STRETCHERS:**

1. Modify your nutritional plan for different body requirements: because of age, activity, situation (e.g., pregnancy).

2. Plan a week's menu, taking into account special situations (e.g., birthdays, restaurants).

3. Examine and compare the nutritional values of fast food options.

4. Compare the cost of menus and devise a low-budget and a high-budget version.

5. Convert calories into other forms of energy.

6. Make comparisons between animal and human energy output.

DUGOUT

A cheeseburger contains about 30 grams of fat. To get the same amount of fat, how much of each of the following would you have to eat: broccoli, pasta, pears?

80 cups of broccoli, 30 cups of pasta, 45 pears (PDR 1995, 156).

The Lion King's Timon says that termite meat has roughly twice the protein of sirloin steak.

The Bouncing Ball of Weight

TEACHER PLAY BOOK

☑ **ACTIVITY DESCRIPTION:** Students develop a weight control plan.

☑ **SPORTS:** Physiology, training for all

☑ **MATHEMATICAL STRAND OUTCOMES:** Students will:
- accurately calculate percentages and ratios
- mathematically derive correlations
- represent data in pie chart and spreadsheet form

☑ **INFORMATION LITERACY OUTCOMES:** Students will:
- locate information about weight control
- determine main ideas from sources

☑ **PREREQUISITE SKILLS:**
- basic calculation skills
- basic spreadsheet skills

☑ **RATIONALE FOR THE ACTIVITY:** Teens are very aware of social messages about weight. With the added role— and possible stress— of sports, teens feel a real need to get in shape. Caught in the "image" and "quick-fix" traps, they may use unhealthy or unproven methods. This activity helps them see how the body uses caloric energy so they can make healthy choices about weight.

☑ **COACHING TIPS:** Because students may be sensitive about weight issues, allow them to create their own scenario. (This can actually lead to fun results!) Students may calculate changes manually, but learning how to use a spreadsheet is a valuable exercise. If some students know how to calculate formulas with a spreadsheet software program, they may be paired with those who don't, thus encouraging peer coaching.

WARM-UPS

1. Comparing apples and pears: pear-shaped people have less chance of getting cardiovascular diseases (such as heart attacks) than do people with big tummies. A simple ratio is a tip-off: waist/hip greater than .8 for women, and greater than 1.0 for men means trouble. How do you measure? Find your waist circumference at its narrowest point (don't suck in); measure your hip circumference at its widest point (where you stick out).

   a. Find your ratio. Compare it with other members of your family. Are there any patterns?

   b. Why do you think the two genders have different ratios?

2. A *Calorie* is the amount of energy it takes to raise the temperature of 1 kilogram of water 1°C. It takes 3,500 calories to make a pound of fat. If you eat an extra 900 calories a day, how long will it take to gain a pound of fat?

   a. If you burn 200 extra calories a day (say, by roller-blading 30 minutes), how long will it take to lose 1 pound of fat?

   b. Create a graph showing the combination of ways to lose 10 pounds in 10 days. Note: a teenage girl needs 2,300 calories per day; a boy needs 3,000 (2,800 for a preteen). Determine a safe solution.

3. Another consideration in determining ideal weight is to reduce the body's fat mass; 20% is a safe number. If a person has a fat mass of 30% and weighs 200 pounds, how much weight would he or she have to lose (understanding the need to exercise to get to this point)? (Hint: to derive lean body mass [LBM], subtract the fat mass from the total weight.)

4. The *Basal Metabolic Rate* (BMR) is the energy you need to live (even in a coma). It's about 60% of an adult's caloric use. If a woman eats 2,000 calories a day, how many calories are used for other activity?

a. As preteens and teens grow, their BMR rises. Muscle mass also increases BMR because keeping muscles toned takes energy. On top of that, the body adjusts to body fat changes, so teens can eat more and still be fit, and blitz dieters may lower their BMR and find it harder to maintain weight loss *and* muscle tone. The latter situation can play out this way: say a woman decides to lose weight by eating less as follows:

Week	Weight in Pounds	BMR
0	120 (25% of weight is fat)	1,000
1	116 (1.2 lbs fat, 2.5 lbs glycogen)	800
2	113 (1 lb fat, 2 lbs muscle—no glycogen left)	700
3	110 (1 lb fat, 2 lbs muscle)	650

At week three, what percentage of her weight is fat? In what probable shape are her muscles? What do you think will happen if she goes back to her regular diet?

STUDENT GAME PLAN

☑ **CONTEXT:** So you want to be — or keep — in shape. But what shape is that? Is it a matter of cutting out snacks or junk food? Do pills help? Do you need to run 10 miles a day? Do sports make a difference? How about just throwing up after every meal? It's a weighty problem. What *is* known is that weight is a function of bones, muscles, and fat. Normally, the trick is to normalize the fat ratio (through healthy eating) and the Basal Metabolic Rate (through exercise).

☑ **CHALLENGE:** You are a sports trainer. Your job is to help your budding athlete get into shape in terms of weight. Create a healthy plan that he or she can follow.

☑ **TASKS:**

1. Choose a person: imaginary or real — even yourself.
2. Measure the person's present health condition: weight and hourly exercise/activity.
3. Consulting weight charts, determine what his or her weight should be.
4. Research activity/sports and exercise charts to determine the daily calorie burn rate.
5. Devise a weekly plan to get him or her into shape.

☑ **RESOURCES:** Sources of information on calories, weight control, exercise, sports.

☑ **ASSESSMENT:** Your final project should include two pie charts (present and ideal daily activity, each labeled with calorie expenditures); a chart showing present and ideal health conditions; and a spreadsheet showing daily and weekly totals for calorie intake (food) and outgo (exercise), weight, and other health measurements. You will be assessed on the accuracy and thoroughness of your plan, your process for devising the plan, and concluding reflections.

☑ **STRETCHERS:**

1. Devise a health plan for people in different types of situations: anorexic, pregnant, newborn, aged, recovering from surgery.
2. Devise an *un*healthy plan, and describe what will happen to the person physically.
3. There are several commercial weight programs, and all have costs associated with them (*PDR* 1995, 104–105):

   - Weight Watchers: $15 to $20 signup fee, $9 to $12 each meeting (weekly), $2 to $4 per Weight Watcher meal (optional); lose 1.5 to 2 pounds per week average.

- Jenny Craig: $79 registration, $60 to $70 food per week (cost drops when you approach your goal and can eat regular food), $2.25 vitamins per week, $99 per year for weight maintenance fees, $75 counseling tape (optional); lose 2 to 3 pounds per week average.

- Nutri-System: $79 enrollment, $69 food per week (when halfway to your goal it's $49 per week); lose 1.5 to 2 pounds per week average.

- Diet Center: $52 to $79 enrollment, $37 to $53 per week reducing phase, $110 weight maintenance (no time limit), $2 to $4 per Diet Center meal (optional); lose 2 pounds per week average.

   a. Graph the relative weekly cost for each option (indicate the range in cost from low end to high end).

   b. Choose the amount of pounds to lose, and determine which program is the most cost-effective.

4. A page on the Internet advertises a growth hormone oral spray: weight loss in a bottle. In a study they proclaim results of 14.4% fat loss and 8.8% increased lean muscle mass. They also tout anabolic improvement and wrinkle reduction. Determine the validity of these claims. (This is a real ad.) Investigate other weight loss "quick fixes."

DUGOUT

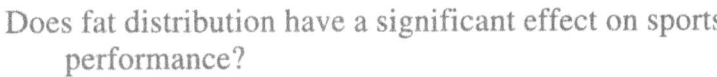

Does fat distribution have a significant effect on sports performance?

No, but added fat does affect motion mechanics, so performance is worse.

Are men much more powerful than women at the same weight?

Although there's a 12% difference, once body fat is factored in, the difference is only about 3%.

The Body Machine

TEACHER PLAY BOOK

☑ **ACTIVITY DESCRIPTION:** Students investigate how body movements demonstrate different physics concepts.

☑ **SPORTS:** Physiology, training for all

☑ **MATHEMATICAL STRAND OUTCOMES:** Students will:
- identify and explain different orders of levers
- measure and calculate force and power functions
- calculate vectors (optional)
- represent data in model or pictorial form

☑ **INFORMATION LITERACY OUTCOMES:** Students will:
- locate information about exercise and its physical components
- interpret visual information
- translate physical properties into physics concepts

☑ **PREREQUISITE SKILLS:**
- basic knowledge about simple machines
- ability to calculate vectors (optional)
- collaborative work

☑ **RATIONALE FOR THE ACTIVITY:** The body can be considered a complex machine. Regardless of the sport, students need to use their own equipment — their bodies — properly. This activity helps students use the mathematical principles of work and energy to calculate their own force and power to their best advantage.

☑ **COACHING TIPS:** Start by discussing different types of machines, and identify the three orders of levers. Using a large picture of the body (or a willing student), have students identify different movements of the body, such as around each joint. Then have student triads research the forces involved in each movement. Students may have a difficult time conceptualizing different types of physical "machines." Using simple props such as rulers, erasers (load), and pencil grips (fulcrum), students can experience the different orders of levers firsthand. Alternatively, students may use Interactive Physics software or similar products to "virtually" test force fields. Students should also be encouraged to make drawings of the force fields. Because velocity is speed plus direction, you may want to limit discussion of velocity to one-directional speed. Mathematically sophisticated students should explore force using vector analysis, which would take into account changes in direction to calculate true velocity.

WARM-UPS

1. An Olympic athlete can lift 500 pounds from floor to extended arms overhead (7 feet) in .8 second. A power lifter takes 2 seconds to lift 1,000 pounds 2.5 feet. If one-directional velocity = distance divided by time, power = force times velocity, and weight may be substituted for force in this situation, which athlete is more powerful?

   a. If work = force times distance, which athlete is doing more work?

   b. What is the correlation between work and power? Where does strength come in?

2. *Horsepower* is defined as the rate at which a horse can work. James Watt calculated it to be about 550 foot-pounds per second. So a horse could raise a 275-pound weight 2 feet per second. The function is P(hp) = W (ft-lb.)/(550 times t [sec]).

   a. At how many horsepower are the athletes in exercise 1 working?

   b. Do you think the phrase "to work as hard as a horse" is realistic? Why?

58   The Body Machine

- ☑ **CONTEXT:** It's been said that the body is a machine. Your muscles, which comprise two-fifths of your body weight, make movement possible and give you the strength to perform well in sports. In physics, a *machine* is "any device by which energy can be transferred from one place to another or one form to another" (Freeman 1990, 45). Hitting a ball, lifting a weight, or even going up the stairs is machine work. If *work* is defined as force times distance (W = fd), then you could say that sports is a lot of work. Fortunately, work divided by time is power (P = W/t), so the faster you run or lift, the more powerful you are. Does that mean if you do your math homework in less time, you are a more powerful student? (Only if you get the answers right!)

- ☑ **CHALLENGE:** Engineer your own sports training. Investigate the power of different body movements and exercises, and determine which kind of exercise would be the most work and the most powerful for the sport of your choice.

- ☑ **TASKS:**
    1. Form a triad team: one expert for each order of lever.
    2. Choose one sport.
    3. Research movements related to that sport. Determine the kinds of simple machine principles used by the body (e.g., what order of lever).
    4. Calculate representative functions of work and power related to the movements.
    5. Diagram the movements in terms of the force involved.
    6. With another team, compare the two sets of movements and related functions.

- ☑ **RESOURCES:** Sources of information on machines, physics, exercise, and sports; physics software (optional); supplies or software for diagramming; equipment for testing levers (optional).

- ☑ **ASSESSMENT:** Your final product should include a series of diagrams representing different movements related to your chosen sport and mathematical calculations of the related work and power, and an analysis of the comparative movements and mathematical findings of your sport and another sport. You will be assessed on the accuracy and thoroughness of your diagrams and mathematical calculations, as well as your comparative analysis.

☑ STRETCHERS:

1. Investigate the relationships among force, strength, and power.

2. Research records on sports efforts (e.g., weight-lifting, throwing speeds) and calculate the relative power and work for each.

3. Convert sports power and work measurements into other units, and compare them to manmade machinery measurements.

DUGOUT

What's the main balancing point for body movement?

The pelvis; it's the main source of power.

By the way, only well-trained athletes can work at 1 horsepower for more than a few seconds. So you might work like a horse, but not for long.

Getting Pumped

TEACHER PLAY BOOK

☑ **ACTIVITY DESCRIPTION:** Students investigate the physiological aspects of exercise and factors affecting performance.

☑ **SPORTS:** Training for all

☑ **MATHEMATICAL STRAND OUTCOMES:** Students will:
- calculate functions related to physiology and exercise
- identify independent and dependent variables
- determine correlations between performance and outside factors
- represent data in graph form

☑ **INFORMATION LITERACY OUTCOMES:**
- locate and assess information about exercise and physiology
- determine significant facts

☑ **PREREQUISITE SKILLS:**
- basic calculation skills
- basic graphing skills
- collaborative work

☑ **RATIONALE FOR THE ACTIVITY:** Exercise is obviously beneficial, but its energy output and physiological impact are often unknown. In this activity, students apply their measurement and functions skills to calculate fitness, and factor in outside variables. In the process, they discover that getting ready for peak performance is mathematically and physically a function of several factors.

☑ **COACHING TIPS:** To focus the class, have them brainstorm ways that the body is affected during exercise, such as heat generation, blood pressure, water loss (sweat), heart rate, and oxygen consumed. Divide the class into small cooperative teams to research the functions related to the measure. Each team member can focus on one variable, such as body condition or intensity of exercise; students may need help in thinking of variables that would change the quantities in the function. Next, have students brainstorm outside factors that would affect performance during exercise, such as gym equipment, extreme temperature, extreme altitude, humidity, pollution, clothing. Divide students into new collaborative teams, with one representative from each of the original teams (this is called a *jigsaw* approach) to research the effects on the exercise previously explored. If possible, have students use graphing calculators or software throughout the activity.

WARM-UPS

1. Cardiac output (the amount of blood pumped by the heart per minute) equals the stroke volume (the volume pumped for each heartbeat) times the heart rate (number of heartbeats per minute). At rest, the average adult's rates are 70 milliliters per beat stroke volume and 70 beats per minute. What is the cardiac output?

    a. For a sedentary person, exercise can raise the stroke volume to 113 milliliters per beat and 195 beats per minute. What is the cardiac output?

    b. A trained athlete can raise the stroke volume to 179 milliliters per beat at the same heart rate. What is the difference in percentage in cardiac output between the two persons?

2. There are two energy types of exercise: *aerobic* and *anaerobic*. Anaerobic, which doesn't use oxygen, is short-term, high-intensity activity. Most moderate exercise is aerobic. Here are some energy-related data for sports:

Sport	Time	Calories/Hour	% Anaerobic/ % Aerobic
400-meter sprint	1 min	900	50/50
basketball	1-min bouts	500	20/80
speed-cycling	1 hr	750	2/98

What conclusions can you draw from these data?

3. A sweat loss of more than 7% of body weight can lead to circulation problems and possibly death. In extreme heat, marathon runners have been known to sweat up to 6 liters of water per hour. What would be the percentage of body weight lost by a 150-pound runner?

62 Getting Pumped

STUDENT GAME PLAN

☑ **CONTEXT:** Want to get in shape? Exercise! Want to be the best in sports? Train! Basically, training is a long-term planned exercise program that usually has specific goals. In either case, the body is working hard. If you add outside factors, such as equipment or environment, your body can really be challenged.

☑ **CHALLENGE:** Assume that you are coaching an Olympic team. Assess the changes in the body when exercised. Then "put on the heat" by finding out how outside factors affect the body's performance, based on the site of the Olympic games.

☑ **TASKS:**

1. Choose one measure of body change in exercise, such as heart rate.
2. Research the impact of exercise.
3. Derive or find mathematical functions describing the effect.
4. Determine how the measurement could change; for example, heart rate could vary depending on the type of exercise (bowling vs. speed-cycling).
5. Each team member calculates the effect for a different variable and graphs the findings.
6. Share the findings within your team and then summarize the findings for the class.
7. Regroup. Your new team consists of one member from each of the original teams.
8. Choose a physically challenging Olympic site, such as Mexico City or Oslo. (If you pick a site that has already been used for the Games, it is easier to research its impact on athletic performance. However, an original site can be more fun to work with, such as New Delhi during the monsoon season.)
9. Research the possible associated variables that would affect performance. For example, extreme altitude could mean lower air pressure, so distance running would be more difficult and high-jumping would be easier.
10. Recalculate and regraph those measures, with each team member focusing on one event.
11. Suggest ways your athletes can prepare for the site's challenges.

From: Go Figure! Mathematics Through Sports. © 1999 Lesley S. J. Farmer. Teacher Ideas Press. 1-800-237-6124.

☑ **RESOURCES:** Sources of information on exercise, training, and physiology; graphing software or calculators (optional).

☑ **ASSESSMENT:** Your final project should include three parts: a series of functions and graphs for one measurement of exercise, a series of functions and graphs for one Olympic site, and a training plan for peak performance. You will be assessed on the mathematical rigor and accuracy of your functions and graphs and on the feasibility of your training plan.

☑ **STRETCHERS:**

1. Investigate the impact of exercise on different populations: young children, the aged, gender-linked.

2. Apply the same process to the Special Olympics.

DUGOUT

Give me air! For exercise that requires 4 liters of air per minute, muscle oxygen consumption rate is almost 70 times that when resting.

Oh, My Aching Back!

TEACHER PLAY BOOK

☑ **ACTIVITY DESCRIPTION:** Students analyze sports injuries.

☑ **SPORTS:** Physiology, all

☑ **MATHEMATICAL STRAND OUTCOMES:** Students will:
- derive statistics from data on sports injuries
- represent data in diagram and graphical form
- make predictions about body impact based on data analysis
- calculate force and related functions (optionally, using vector analysis)

☑ **INFORMATION LITERACY OUTCOMES:**
- locate information about sports injuries and physiology
- interpret graphical information
- correlate information on injuries to physiology

☑ **PREREQUISITE SKILLS:**
- basic statistical skills
- basic graphing skills
- basic physiology knowledge
- basic knowledge of mechanical laws

☑ **RATIONALE FOR THE ACTIVITY:** Teenagers are most at risk for injuries, even with the best supervision. By studying the statistics on injuries and determining the causes for them, students become more aware of potential hazards and more capable of controlling for those factors. The mathematical component provides an objective approach, and the resulting calculations of the amount of force and torque can be, literally, very powerful.

☑ **COACHING TIPS:** Students may need additional information about force, torque, and other mechanical laws. Mathematically sophisticated students should analyze injuries using vector analysis, taking into consideration issues such as torque and acceleration. A useful visualizing tool is Interactive Physics software, which enables students to set up physical conditions and then see what happens.

# WARM-UPS

1. The average jogger's foot hits the ground about 3,000 times per mile. Since the force of landing is about three times a person's weight (because you usually have only one foot on the ground at a time), what would be the total amount of force in a mile? Why do you think the major injury in jogging is "runner's knee"?

   a. Thick-soled shoes can reduce body impact by 30% over thin-soled shoes. What would be the difference in force?

   b. Thick-soled shoes result in greater torque (rotational force around an axis—the ankle). So if a player has weak ankles, thin-soled shoes with ankle braces, or high-tops, are recommended. Explain the rationale. (Which would you rather have: runner's knee or ankle sprain?)

2. The two sports with the lowest rates of injury in the United States are bowling and curling; the highest rate is for skeet-shooting. Why?

   a. More than 90% of U.S. children who use playground equipment get injured; fewer than .5% are injured playing rugby. Why?

 STUDENT GAME PLAN

- ☑ **CONTEXT:** The leading cause of death and disease among school-aged children is unintentional injury. Almost 40% of all injuries happen to kids younger than 15, mainly to young teenagers (Southmayd and Hoffman 1981, 18). Even so, sports are becoming safer each year because of preventative measures: safer equipment, rules, and behaviors.

- ☑ **CHALLENGE:** What is the situation with sports injuries? By analyzing the data, you can help prevent those injuries. For instance, because injuries to the face and head used to make up about a third of all bicycle injuries, many schools and some states have instituted helmet laws (the correlation is even more striking when analyzing the numbers relative to those bikers wearing headgear or not). Find out what injuries are common to individual sports, and determine the reasons and possible injury prevention measures.

- ☑ **TASKS:**
    1. Choose a sport.
    2. Research injuries associated with the sport.
    3. Generate and graph statistics related to sports injuries.
    4. Analyze the injury data to determine which body functions are associated with the injuries.
    5. Calculate the forces related to the injured parts of the body.
    6. Based on mathematical analysis and research in the sport, suggest ways to prevent or minimize injuries.

- ☑ **RESOURCES:** Sources of information on sports, injuries, statistics, physics, and physiology; Interactive Physics software to test forces (optional).

- ☑ **ASSESSMENT:** Your final project should consist of a statistical analysis of the sport injury; diagrams of the forces involved in each of the body's injuries, with mathematical evidence; and recommendations for injury prevention or minimization based on data analysis. You will be assessed on the accuracy and thoroughness of your findings and the mathematical rigor of your recommendations.

- ☑ **STRETCHERS:**
    1. Compare injuries across sports.
    2. Focus on one body part, and analyze injuries to the body across sports.
    3. Research the physiological effects of drugs on the body.

 **DUGOUT**

What four sports account for the majority of injuries?
Bicycling, baseball, football, and basketball.

Marathon: Go for the Gold!

TEACHER PLAY BOOK

- ☑ **ACTIVITY DESCRIPTION:** Students develop a physical fitness/training program.

- ☑ **SPORTS:** Physiology, training for all

- ☑ **MATHEMATICAL STRAND OUTCOMES:** Students will:
  - calculate energy-related functions
  - identify and explain mathematical correlations
  - make predictions about changes in the body based on modifications
  - represent data in a variety of ways

- ☑ **INFORMATION LITERACY OUTCOMES:** Students will:
  - locate information on physical fitness, training, and physics
  - determine the main facts from sources
  - analyze information to make informed decisions
  - organize and present information in appropriate formats

- ☑ **PREREQUISITE SKILLS:**
  - calculation skills
  - graphing skills
  - collaborative work

- ☑ **RATIONALE FOR THE ACTIVITY:** Getting into shape for peak performance is a long-term, complex task. It requires control and interdependence of body composition as well as body conditioning—and is influenced by outside factors as well. This culminating activity helps students to synthesize concepts of physical fitness as well as to apply the mathematics of functions and data analysis. An explanation of each decision and its consequences is vital to demonstrate understanding. The journal form of the project helps personalize and concretize the program.

- ☑ **COACHING TIPS:** Students may use their findings from previous activities to help them develop a well-rounded fitness/training program. To help them focus, have the class review the elements of a fitness/training program. What measurements should be taken? What correlations exist between variables? How is fitness a function of specific actions? Students may also want to brainstorm possible outside variables that would require the plan to change, such as accident, illness, pregnancy, climate, or finances. Students may want to group themselves by sport or level of achievement, for example personal fitness, interscholastic sports, Olympic training, or professional sports. Encourage them to research existing training programs. As a culminating activity, have teams compare the training programs and draw conclusions from their investigation.

# STUDENT GAME PLAN

☑ **CONTEXT:** So you want to be an Olympic gold medal–winner or a professional athlete — or, at least, reach your peak performance and physical fitness. They are worthy goals that demand a well-developed program to be followed faithfully. There is no overnight success, but a sense of well-being and the establishment of healthy lifelong habits can't be beat. You can be a winner every time! You might even consider becoming a personal trainer: the money can be great, you can stay in the business a long time, and you'll sustain fewer injuries.

☑ **CHALLENGE:** Be a personal trainer for yourself or for another person. Consider all the elements of a good program as you develop and follow the plan. Calculate changes over time. Include at least two events that would change the program and show the impact of those factors. In journal form, explain how performance and fitness change as the program progresses.

☑ **TASKS:**

1. Choose a person, real or imagined. Generate baseline mathematical data on him or her.
2. Determine a goal based on a specific sport.
3. Research the physical demands needed to achieve in the sport; find out what similar training programs exist.
4. Develop a fitness/training program that includes nutrition and exercise.
5. Determine and calculate the data needed to assess the program. Chart it on a weekly basis for at least two months.
6. Introduce at least two outside variables that would affect the program. Modify the program as needed, calculate the changes, and chart them.
7. In journal form, discuss the impact of the program in terms of physical fitness and performance. Be specific.

☑ **RESOURCES:** Sources of information on training, physical fitness, sports, and physics; spreadsheet software (or manual ledger); calculator (optional).

☑ **ASSESSMENT:** Your final project should include the fitness/training program, spreadsheets, graphs as applicable, and a journal. You will be assessed on the healthiness and thoroughness of your plan, the accuracy of your calculations, and the rationale of your journal explanation.

# DUGOUT

Keep on pumping! People who don't exercise regularly lose muscular strength. By age 65, you could lose up to 80% of your original strength.

Part IV
Knowing the Ropes

Knowing Your Limits

TEACHER PLAY BOOK

- ☑ **ACTIVITY DESCRIPTION:** Students compare the playing fields of different sports.

- ☑ **SPORTS:** Most

- ☑ **MATHEMATICAL STRAND OUTCOMES:** Students will:
  - calculate perimeter, area, and volume
  - represent data in scatterplot form
  - draw conclusions about perimeter, area, and volume from scatterplots

- ☑ **INFORMATION LITERACY OUTCOMES:** Students will:
  - locate information about playing fields
  - interpret visual information

- ☑ **PREREQUISITE SKILLS:**
  - basic graphing skills
  - basic calculation skills

- ☑ **RATIONALE FOR THE ACTIVITY:** This activity helps students see the relationships among playing fields while practicing geometric calculations with real-life applications. They should also see the relationship between perimeter, area, and volume.

- ☑ **COACHING TIPS:** Encourage students to be creative by considering elliptical or 3D space.

WARM-UPS

1. Basketball court dimensions vary according to the level of play: for the NBA/NCAA it is 50 by 94 feet; FIBA is 49 feet, 2.5 inches by 91 feet, 10 inches; and high school is 50 by 84 feet. What is the perimeter and area relationship among the three courts?

2. A one-wall racquetball court is 20 by 34 feet with a 16-foot-high wall. What is the volume of the playing "field"?

STUDENT GAME PLAN

- ☑ **CONTEXT:** Playing area helps define a sport not only because of lines, such as the 50-yard one, but because it helps determine what kind of action occurs. Ping-Pong, for instance, would be vastly different on a football field.

- ☑ **CHALLENGE:** You need to mark a multipurpose room for as many games as possible in the smallest amount of space. Assume that the floor composition doesn't matter (for example, you can play football and tennis on the same flooring).

- ☑ **TASKS:**
    1. Find out the playing space for 20 sports.
    2. Make a scatterplot graph, length by width, to compare playing spaces.
    3. Draw conclusions about the playing spaces based on the data.
    4. Determine the smallest space needed for playing all the chosen sports.
    5. Determine the least number of lines and draw them as needed to define the playing spaces. (Remember to include the inner lines.)

- ☑ **RESOURCES:** Sources of information on sports, such as rule books; graphing supplies or software.

- ☑ **ASSESSMENT:** Your final project should consist of a scatterplot graph, a model of the multipurpose room, and a mathematical analysis. You will be assessed on the thoroughness and accuracy of your representations and on the mathematical rigor of the conclusions derived from the data.

- ☑ **STRETCHERS:**
    1. Calculate how to make maximum use of a Roman coliseum.
    2. Follow the same process for board games.
    3. Calculate how much paint would be needed to paint the lines in the above activity.
    4. Calculate spaces for elliptical fields, such as tracks.

DUGOUT

The largest bowling center in the world was the Tokyo World Lanes Center. It had 252 lanes.

What's the Score?

TEACHER PLAY BOOK

☑ **ACTIVITY DESCRIPTION:** Students create a game to identify feasible sports scores.

☑ **SPORTS:** All

☑ **MATHEMATICAL STRAND OUTCOMES:** Students will:
- identify realistic numerical combinations
- offer mathematical reasons for numerical combinations
- make predictions based on numerical information

☑ **INFORMATION LITERACY OUTCOMES:** Students will:
- locate information about sports scores
- classify information

☑ **PREREQUISITE SKILLS:**
- basic computational skills

☑ **RATIONALE FOR THE ACTIVITY:** What is a reasonable number? It depends on the context. This activity helps students to calculate possible number combinations for games and to make predictions based on their calculations.

☑ **COACHING TIPS:** To focus students, have them generate a list of possible sports. Try having each student calculate scores for one game he or she enjoys, and for one game he or she does not know. This stretch encourages students to do research in a new area. The more familiar students are with a game, the more likely they will be able to generate logical numerical combinations. Also try to distribute scores so that no one has two sports with high scores (such as basketball) or two sports with low scores (such as hockey). If the class runs out of games, include variations for different levels of playing, such as football, or have students work in pairs with one or two sports. Note that scores will differ according to the level of play: Little League baseball scores would differ greatly from major league plays. Students may need to increase the size of their slips of paper (or decrease their handwriting size) as the numbers increase; this is a good hands-on exploratory corollary on number combinations.

From: *Go Figure! Mathematics Through Sports.* © 1999 Lesley S. J. Farmer. Teacher Ideas Press. 1-800-237-6124.

WARM-UPS

1. In what sport would 100 be a good score? In what sport would 100 be a poor score?

2. How many different ways can a football team make seven points?

STUDENT GAME PLAN

☑ **CONTEXT:** If someone says their team won a game 2 to 1, would you be elated or let-down? It depends; it could have been a riveting baseball game or a horrific basketball game. If someone says their football team totaled 30 points, would you know what plays were made? Scores can be amazingly ambiguous.

☑ **CHALLENGE:** Create a game based on sports scores. The more creative you are, the better!

☑ **TASKS:**

1. Choose two sports: one you know well and one you don't know at all (how about quoits or snooker?). Make sure one has high points (say, golf) and one has lower points (such as gymnastics).

2. Research the scoring system for your sports and create a score card for each.

3. Initial and number a set of paper slips from 1 to 100 (or whatever your top score would be), and decide whether that number could exist as a score for your sport. Write all the possible combinations for a score on the back of the slip. For example, a 10 in football could be derived from a converted touchdown and a field goal, a touchdown and two safeties, or two field goals and two safeties.

4. Now you're ready to play the game. Display the scorecards for class referral. (You can make it harder by *not* showing the cards.) A student picks a number from 1 to 100 (or whatever the highest reasonable number for a sport). You and the rest of the class then try to come up with a logical combination that matches that number; state the sport and how the number can be formed according to the scoring system. It doesn't have to be in the sport you researched, but it's obviously easier for that sport. You can also bluff by giving the wrong combination or sport. If you are right, you get a point; if you bluff and get away with it, you gain a point and the picker loses a point; if you're caught in the bluff, you lose a point and the picker gains a point. The person who researched the particular sport is the final arbiter (the one who says whether the combination is correct or not). The class gains a point for every correct combination for a particular number. The game can be played in teams, partners, or individually. The goal is to get the highest class points and highest individual or team points.

☑ **RESOURCES:** Sources of information on sports scoring systems, slips of paper for each student, a random number generator, recording supplies (such as markers and newsprint).

☑ **ASSESSMENT:** Your final project should include your list of scores and accompanying combinations. The game is the culminating event. You will be assessed on the accuracy and quantity of combinations.

☑ **STRETCHERS:**

1. Calculate how many combinations of scores are possible for a particular sport.
2. Create new games and scoring systems.

DUGOUT

It's a close one: Sweden beat the United States in the 1972 men's 400-meter individual medley by .002 second. Nowadays, timings are determined only to hundredths.

Collide Scope

TEACHER PLAY BOOK

- ☑ **ACTIVITY DESCRIPTION:** Students analyze the force of collision in sports.

- ☑ **SPORTS:** All that involve colliding (either on purpose or accidental)

- ☑ **MATHEMATICAL STRAND OUTCOMES:** Students will:
  - calculate collision forces
  - graph a series of data
  - compare data mathematically

- ☑ **INFORMATION LITERACY OUTCOMES:** Students will:
  - locate information on energy and sports
  - determine relevant collision and energy forces

- ☑ **PREREQUISITE SKILLS:**
  - ability to use functions
  - graphing skills
  - ability to convert measurement units

- ☑ **RATIONALE FOR THE ACTIVITY:** Collisions can be very dramatic to watch. This visceral impact can be used to help students quantify physical force in sports.

- ☑ **COACHING TIPS:** Focus the class by having them describe collisions or physical impacts (e.g., karate board-breaking) they have observed in sports. You might want to have them guess the relative amount of force in each collision, and then compare those figures to the final ones they derive. This activity works well in pairs: one calculates household power, and the other calculates sports energy.

WARM-UPS

1. Two football players collide. One weighs 250 pounds and runs 7 yards per second. The other weighs 200 pounds and runs 8 yards per second. If kinetic energy = 1/2 mv², where m = mass and v = velocity, what is the energy of each player when he collides? Whose is greater?

   a. The total energy of the collision is the sum of the two bodies. What is the energy amount in joules? (Hint: 2.2 lbs = 1 kg; 1 ft = 0.3048 m; 1 J = 0.75 ft/lb)

   b. 1 watt = 1 joule of energy per second. Assuming the collision time is a quarter of a second, how many 60-watt lightbulbs could burn in that amount of time?

2. Sumo wrestlers don't run the same distances that football players do. Basically, momentum (mass times velocity) is the main physics formula involved: going from inertia to an accelerating force to collision (when momentum decreases). If both wrestlers move at the same speed, who wins?

   a. If wrestler Ashi weighs 180 kilograms and wrestler Bashi weighs 250 kilograms, how much faster does Ashi have to go in order to win (i.e., drive the other one out of the 7-foot ring)?

# STUDENT GAME PLAN

☑ **CONTEXT:** Demolition races. The crack of football helmets. A skier dies from colliding with a tree. Sports can be dangerous. And energetic, both figuratively and literally.

☑ **CHALLENGE:** You live in Eerie, Indiana, the local sports capital. Thanks to a bat getting fried in the power lines, there's no more electricity and the generators have been knocked out. Now the only way to get power is to induce sports collisions, which magically convert to household power. Calculate how many sports collisions are necessary (and how often) to keep each home "cooking."

☑ **TASKS:**

1. Choose a sport that involves collisions.
2. Research representative figures for collisions.
3. Research representative figures for household use of energy.
4. Calculate collision and household energy in terms of feasible ranges.
5. Plot graphs to describe these figures.
6. Determine the nature of collisions needed to supply a household in terms of energy.
7. Compare and analyze your figures with another pair's.
8. Present a collision energy plan.

☑ **RESOURCES:** Sources of information on energy, sports, and collisions; graphing calculators or software (optional).

☑ **ASSESSMENT:** Your final project should include collision and energy graphs and an energy analysis. You will be assessed on the scientific soundness of your figures, the thoroughness and accuracy of your graphs, and the mathematical rigor of your plan.

☑ **STRETCHERS:**

1. Develop a class chart comparing the relative energy associated with each kind of collision.
2. Calculate the range of feasible energy outputs from collisions.
3. Compare collision energy to other forms of energy.

 **DUGOUT**

The collision between two football players is enough energy to lift a compact car 2 feet into the air (Davis 1997, 58).

Projecting Yourself

TEACHER PLAY BOOK

☑ **ACTIVITY DESCRIPTION:** Students find the optimal conditions for projectiles.

☑ **SPORTS:** Those involving projectiles: badminton, baseball, basketball, tennis and other racquet sports, archery, volleyball, shot put, etc.

☑ **MATHEMATICAL STRAND OUTCOMES:** Students will:
- calculate trajectories
- determine the optimum conditions for projectiles (optionally, using linear programming)
- represent data in graph form

☑ **INFORMATION LITERACY OUTCOMES:** Students will:
- locate information about projectiles
- determine critical factors from data
- collaborative work

☑ **PREREQUISITE SKILLS:**
- graphing skills
- algebraic skills
- basic trigonometric skills
- vector calculations (optional)

☑ **RATIONALE FOR THE ACTIVITY:** Several sports involve launching an object. Each sport's projectile has different quantities to be calculated, but the underlying trigonometric functions and physical principles remain constant. This activity enables students to test these physical properties and improve their performance both on and off the court.

☑ **COACHING TIPS:** To focus the class, have them generate a list of sports that involve projectiles. Then have them brainstorm factors that influence trajectories: launching force, angle, height, characteristics of the projectile, air resistance, etc. This activity works well in pairs or triads. Students should be encouraged to use graphing calculators so they can test hypotheses more easily.

WARM-UPS

1. If you throw a ball horizontally or drop it from 32 feet up, it will hit the ground at the same time (1 second) because of gravity. If, however, a ball is launched at 45° 32 feet up at a launching speed of 100 mph, the distance is calculated at $(v^2 \sin 2\theta)/g$, where v = launching speed and g = acceleration of gravity or 32 ft/sec^2. When will it land and how far will it travel horizontally?

2. Basketball hoops are now 10 feet high. Feasibly, counting the combined height of the player and the jump, a player may have only a 6-inch release distance, as opposed to a 24-inch distance for a short player. If the hoop were raised to 12 feet (which has been suggested since 1932), what would be the release distances?

    a. What would be the difference in percentage from the present situation for tall and short players?

3. The terminal speed of a shuttlecock is 15 mph; it's 325 mph for a 16-pound shot (as in shot put). Why?

STUDENT GAME PLAN

☑ **CONTEXT:** "I shot an arrow into the air, and where it fell I knew not where." Doesn't sound like a very astute athlete, does it? There are only three forces acting on that arrow's flight: propelling force, gravity, and air resistance. Thus, with some mathematical calculations you can predict quite accurately where a projectile will land. You can also calculate the best launching angle so you can really make your point.

☑ **CHALLENGE:** Investigate how to optimize the trajectory of a sports projectile.

☑ **TASKS:**

1. Choose a sport that involves a projectile.
2. Research the elements that influence the trajectory.
3. Calculate and graph the optimum trajectory angle.
4. Suggest factors that would influence the trajectory.
5. Mathematically compare your projectile analysis with findings for another projectile.

☑ **RESOURCES:** Sources of information on sports projectiles, trajectories, and physics; graphing calculators or other graphing software (optional).

☑ **ASSESSMENT:** Your final project should consist of a set of mathematical functions, calculations, and graphs describing your projectile; conjectures about trajectory variances; and a mathematical analysis comparing your findings with those for another sport's projectile. You will be assessed on the thoroughness and accuracy of your calculations and graphs and on the mathematical rigor of your conjectures and comparative analysis.

☑ **STRETCHERS:**

1. Investigate the modifications needed to launch an object other than the one intended for a particular sport, such as using a shuttlecock for a shot put competition or substituting a soccer ball for a basketball.
2. Determine the differences in projectile action if the launch were done on the moon.
3. Determine the effect that height of the launching "pad," elasticity, spin, and rebound have on projectiles.

DUGOUT

The record distance for throwing dried cowpats under the 1970 rules is 266 feet, accomplished at the 1981 Mountain Festival in Tehachapi, California.

What a Drag!

TEACHER PLAY BOOK

- ☑ **ACTIVITY DESCRIPTION:** Students explore Bernoulli's Principle in relationship to sports equipment.

- ☑ **SPORTS:** Ball sports (e.g., baseball, bowling); transportation sports (e.g., cycling, auto-racing, hang-gliding, sailing)

- ☑ **MATHEMATICAL STRAND OUTCOMES:** Students will:
    - mathematically interpret and apply Bernoulli's Principle
    - draw conclusions and make predictions based on data derived from Bernoulli's Principle

- ☑ **INFORMATION LITERACY OUTCOMES:** Students will:
    - locate information on sports and Bernoulli's Principle
    - apply Bernoulli's Principle to sports
    - explain Bernoulli's Principle in diagram form

- ☑ **PREREQUISITE SKILLS:**
    - basic calculation skills
    - basic knowledge of air resistance
    - collaborative work

- ☑ **RATIONALE FOR THE ACTIVITY:** Bernoulli's Principle affects sports performance significantly; it explains how air resistance can be minimized. This activity helps students understand its principles and apply them creatively.

- ☑ **COACHING TIPS:** Start by discussing air resistance; have students generate a list of air resistance effects in sports and a list of ways to reduce air resistance or "drag" (e.g., streamlining cars, wearing tight-fitting clothes when cycling). To introduce Bernoulli's Principle, build on students' visceral experiences by having them relate personal experiences about "lift" or curveballs. Only then give the formal definition of Bernoulli's Principle and explain the phenomenon. As with air resistance, have students generate a list of sports that involve Bernoulli's Principle. This activity is effectively done in pairs, as with competing athletes. Sophisticated math students can apply complex calculations; less sophisticated students can focus on qualitative relationships.

# WARM-UPS

1. Why do golf balls have dimples? It was discovered that old, beat-up balls actually flew longer and farther than new ones. Because a golf ball can fly so fast, air resistance force can make for great variability in flight. Dimples carry a turbulent layer of air around the ball so there's less drag; the air on top of the ball can move faster than at the bottom of the ball. In other words, it "lifts." What do you think would happen if you used a dimpled ball or bat?

2. For most cases in sports, Bernoulli's Principle may be stated as p_0 minus p_1 = $P(v_1^2$ minus $v_0^2)/2$, where p = pressure, P = density, v = velocity, 0 = top, and 1 = bottom. If air density is .08 lb/ft^3, velocity is 25 ft/sec.

   a. Would the difference in pressure between the top and bottom of a wing be greater at 1,000 feet above the ground or 1,000 feet under the sea?

   b. If the top velocity is faster than the bottom, what would be the relationship between the top pressure and the bottom pressure?

   c. If a wing is 10 feet across (flat on the bottom) and 1 foot high, on which side is the air velocity probably faster?

   d. Race cars often have "wings" in the back. What is the shape of the wing? Why?

STUDENT GAME PLAN

☑ **CONTEXT:** Remember holding your hand out the window of a moving car? When your hand was perpendicular to the road, the wind pulled your hand back. If your hand was parallel to the road, however, the wind didn't have much effect on it. This is the power of air resistance. Now try this experiment: hold the edge of a piece of paper down next to your chin, with the rest of the paper dangling over your fingers. Now blow hard just above the paper. It should move upward; if you try hard enough, it should rise to a horizontal position. That's Bernoulli's Principle at work: "A moving stream of air or liquid exerts less sidewise pressure than if at rest." That's what makes a plane fly or a ball curve.

☑ **CHALLENGE:** Make way for Bernoulli! Calculate the optimum condition for an athlete to take advantage of Bernoulli's Principle by changing one factor, such as the equipment's angle or surface.

☑ **TASKS:**

1. With a partner, choose a sport.
2. Research the effects of Bernoulli's Principle in your sport.
3. Calculate the optimum way to take advantage of Bernoulli's Principle as the sport now exists.
4. Each partner makes a different change in a piece of sports equipment (e.g., ball surface, sail angle, wing shape) that would improve sports performance because of Bernoulli's Principle.
5. Draw diagrams to explain your analysis.
6. Compare and analyze the results.

☑ **RESOURCES:** Sources of information on Bernoulli's Principle and sports; physics software (optional); CAD software or drawing supplies.

☑ **ASSESSMENT:** Your final project should consist of three diagrams (and supporting calculations) showing Bernoulli's Principle as it is used by competing athletes. You will be assessed on the scientific soundness of your diagram and numbers, the accuracy of your calculations, and the mathematical rigor of your analysis.

☑ **STRETCHERS:**

1. Investigate the effect that ball shape has on sports performance. Explore how performance would change if a soccer ball were used in football, or a bowling ball were used in the hammer throw.
2. Compare Bernoulli's Principle in the air and in water.

3. Design a low-air-resistant piece of sports equipment.

4. Compare the relative spins (revolutions per minute) of different kinds of balls.

5. Compare the relative spins of different baseballs: spitballs, scuffed balls, unstitched balls, curveballs, knuckle balls, fastballs.

6. Investigate the relative impacts of the Magnus effect and Bernoulli's Principle on golf balls.

DUGOUT

Which spins faster: the fastest major league baseball curve or a golf ball?

Even with a 3-iron, a golf ball can spin 8,000 rpm, at least three times that of a curveball.

Going in Circles

TEACHER PLAY BOOK

☑ **ACTIVITY DESCRIPTION:** Students explore the relationship of wheels and rotation to speed and force.

☑ **SPORTS:** Those involving wheels or other rotational movements

☑ **MATHEMATICAL STRAND OUTCOMES:** Students will:
- identify and calculate rotational algorithms
- describe and calculate the mathematical relationships of gears
- explain and calculate forces of motion
- calculate motion in terms of vectors (optional)

☑ **INFORMATION LITERACY OUTCOMES:** Students will:
- locate information about wheels and rotational sports
- identify the rotational forces associated with the sport

☑ **PREREQUISITE SKILLS:**
- basic computational skills
- ability to convert measurements
- basic mechanical knowledge

☑ **RATIONALE FOR THE ACTIVITY:** Youths like speed! But they often don't realize the complexity or force of that motion. This activity helps students understand mechanical principles of gears, revolution, and motion through their knowledge of sports.

☑ **COACHING TIPS:** To focus the class, have them list sports that involve rotation, and have them brainstorm factors that influence speed and force. Remind them that rotational motion doesn't have to involve wheels. The list should at least include: auto-racing, cycling, skating, skateboarding, baseball, golf, and track events. Then incorporate the physical forces that relate to these sports: consider speed, velocity, acceleration, torque, inertia, and angular momentum. Students may need to explore the mechanical principles concretely by testing them on equipment. To simplify the activity, explore only sports using wheels; otherwise, have half the class focus on wheels and half focus on human rotations; then jigsaw the teams to compare the physical forces between sports.

WARM-UPS

1. For two gears to work together, they must have a whole number ratio of gear teeth. If one gear has 12 teeth and the other has 36 teeth, then their ratio is 1:3 and it takes the 12-teeth gear three revolutions to turn the other gear around one time. On a bike, the higher the ratio, the harder it is to pedal; more force is required. But the cyclist goes farther. Why?

   a. If a wheel radius is 12 inches, and the pedal/wheel gear ratio is 5:1, how far would the bike go for every pedal revolution?

   b. If each pedal rotation moves a bike forward 25 feet, at what angular frequency (revolutions/second) would a biker have to go to maintain a speed of 25 mph?

2. Notice that a skater spins more slowly when the arms are extended. Why?

3. In the hammer throw, a 16-pound sphere is attached to a 4-foot-long wire (with a handle on the end). The thrower spins the hammer around himself or herself up to five times and then throws it. The inward pull of the thrower (centripetal force) is calculated at $F = mv^2/r$, where m = mass, v = velocity, and r = radius. If the thrower's arm is a yard long and the speed of the hammer is 64 mph, what is the centripetal force (in pounds)?

   a. If v = distance per revolution times angular frequency, how many revolutions per second must the thrower turn, using the above figures?

   b. At the same time, the hammer is pulling outward with the same amount of force. It should be noted that the thrower launches the hammer at 45°. Therefore, what would be the upward amount of force? If the upward force is greater than the thrower's weight, what will happen?

   c. Experts assert that for every 2.5 centimeters added to the radius, the potential thrown distance can increase 2 meters. What do you think would have greater impact on the distance thrown: arm length, body weight, or muscle strength?

STUDENT GAME PLAN

☑ **CONTEXT:** It's been said that the United States is a nation on wheels; certainly, sports such as cycling and auto-racing are popular. Maybe it's the speed. There's something almost hypnotic about watching skaters spin. What makes the world go round? Perhaps it's a lot of rotational force.

☑ **CHALLENGE:** Take the role of a physical engineer consultant. Identify the various forces of motion for a particular sport and make recommendations on how to capitalize on those forces in order to perform optimally.

☑ **TASKS:**

1. Choose a sport that involves rotation.
2. Identify the physical forces associated with the sport.
3. Research representative quantities associated with the forces.
4. Calculate typical forces for your sport and represent them in diagram form.
5. Determine and calculate force conditions for optimal sports performance.
6. If done as a jigsaw activity, create pairs (one from a wheel sport and one from a human rotation sport). Analyze and compare forces.

☑ **RESOURCES:** Sources of information on physical forces in sports; physics software (optional); sports equipment for experimentation (optional); CAD software or diagramming software; programmable calculators (optional).

☑ **ASSESSMENT:** Your final project will include a force diagram, supporting formulas and calculations, and analysis. You will be assessed on the thoroughness, accuracy, and clarity of your diagram; the appropriateness of your formulas and calculations; and the mathematical rigor of your analysis.

☑ **STRETCHERS:**

1. Investigate the impact of adjusting the rocker angle in in-line skating. Find out why in-line racing skates come with five wheels instead of four.
2. How do wheel design and material affect physical properties?
3. Compare the swings of different sports: golf, baseball, discus throw, etc.

DUGOUT

If a cat is released upside down by his feet a half-meter in the air, he can twist at zero angular momentum and rotate his body to land feet first in .33 second.

Friction Feat

TEACHER PLAY BOOK

☑ **ACTIVITY DESCRIPTION:** Students design equipment that optimizes friction factors in sports performance.

☑ **SPORTS:** All, with a concentration on foot equipment and skating

☑ **MATHEMATICAL STRAND OUTCOMES:** Students will:
- mathematically explain the role of friction in sports performance
- apply physics formulas to shoe design
- change shoe design based on mathematical calculations
- present data in diagram form

☑ **INFORMATION LITERACY OUTCOMES:** Students will:
- locate information on friction, and its influence in sports and on shoes
- identify key features in shoe design and friction influence

☑ **PREREQUISITE SKILLS:**
- ability to use formulas

☑ **RATIONALE FOR THE ACTIVITY:** Students are very aware of shoe design these days, from Air Jordans to cross-trainers. What they might not appreciate, though, is the subtle friction factors between shoes and playing surface. This activity helps students learn more about the impact of surface area and the way that sports take advantage of it.

☑ **COACHING TIPS:** Start the activity by having students discuss the influence that shoes and other equipment (e.g., skis, boards, luges) that works on a surface have on sports performance. Do they think that having the "right" shoe makes a difference? Then have them discuss different playing areas and match those surfaces to shoe types. In presenting their design, they should show how it is an improvement over existing designs. As alternative ways to demonstrate understanding of friction principles, students can design an ineffective shoe and an existing efficient shoe for a particular sport, or they can calculate the frictional impact of using the wrong type of shoe in a particular sport, say golf shoes in basketball or cross-country shoes in football.

WARM-UPS

1. Why do skaters seem to glide on ice? In skating, the amount of fiction is proportional to the ice's upward force on the skater. The *coefficient of friction* is the ratio of friction divided by normal force. So what should happen to lower the coefficient ratio?

    a. Friction slows down skaters, but they need friction to get started, so what would happen if the coefficient ratio was zero?

    b. In contact with the skater's blade, ice melts and forms a thin liquid, which acts as a lubricant. This action is caused by pressure, heat, and *surface melt*: the slightly disordered crystal "edge" of ice. It is thickest at the melting point, 0°C, and thinnest at minus 35°C (.5 nanometer) (Zumerchik 1997, 395). What do you think would be the frictional condition of skating in minus 30° weather?

2. A figure skater might go a constant 20 mph for 2 minutes, while a hockey player might accelerate from 0 to 10 mph six times within the same 2 minutes. Who has to use more energy? Why? Justify your answer mathematically.

3. Friction can be a hindrance or a help. Consider a smooth ramp A that creates 5 pounds of friction, and a rough ramp B that creates 15 pounds of friction. If you pull a 50-pound weight up ramp A, you're actually pulling a total of 105 pounds; up ramp B you pull 115 pounds. But since friction opposes movement, what would be the effective weight you would be lowering on ramp A vs. ramp B? Which ramp would you prefer going up? Which one going down?

STUDENT GAME PLAN

- ☑ **CONTEXT:** *Friction* is the force that resists the motion of one body in contact with another body. In skiing you want little friction; in football you need lots. As a result, shoes (and shoe extensions such as snowboards) are designed to optimize the friction needs of the particular sport. For instance, the new "clapper" shoes in speed-skating resulted in several Olympic speed-skating record-breaking results.

- ☑ **CHALLENGE:** This is your chance to make sports history! Design the perfect sports shoe or transport (e.g., luge, ski) that makes the best use of friction conditions.

- ☑ **TASKS:**
    1. Choose a sport.
    2. Research the friction factor for that sport, focusing on the interaction of foot to playing surface.
    3. Research shoe/transport design in light of the friction factor.
    4. Design the perfect shoe/transport based on mathematical data.
    5. Draw a diagram of the design, showing the relevant friction forces.

- ☑ **RESOURCES:** Sources of information on friction and sports equipment (particularly shoes and transport); CAD software or design supplies.

- ☑ **ASSESSMENT:** Your final project should consist of the design diagram, the mathematics behind the design, and an explanation that demonstrates the design's superiority to existing products. You will be assessed on the feasibility of your design, the accuracy and thoroughness of your calculations, and the persuasiveness of your explanation.

- ☑ **STRETCHERS:**
    1. Trace the history of sports shoes in light of friction factors.
    2. Show mathematically how the wrong shoe can lower performance.

DUGOUT

Nike hoped to sell $10 million in Air Jordan sneakers when they signed on Michael Jordan. After one year they had sold $130 million worth. As for Michael, he received a $2.5 million contract for his endorsement.

What a Racquet!

TEACHER PLAY BOOK

☑ **ACTIVITY DESCRIPTION:** Students investigate the effect of equipment on sports performance.

☑ **SPORTS:** Those involving equipment (tennis is the model)

☑ **MATHEMATICAL STRAND OUTCOMES:** Students will:
- calculate force functions related to the use of sports equipment
- develop working hypotheses
- design a mathematical model for experimentation

☑ **INFORMATION LITERACY OUTCOMES:** Students will:
- locate information on sports equipment
- identify critical features of equipment

☑ **PREREQUISITE SKILLS:**
- ability to calculate vectors (optional)
- basic trigonometric functions (optional)

☑ **RATIONALE FOR THE ACTIVITY:** This activity blends interest in sports equipment with creativity. Students learn how to evaluate equipment mathematically and improve performance through mathematical modeling and prediction.

☑ **COACHING TIPS:** Sophisticated math students can explain the forces using trigonometry and vectors; middle schoolers can show forces by general direction and approximate numerical relations. Students need to look at various aspects of hitting an object: the object's and equipment's weight, the power of the launch, and the physics involved in the interaction of the ball or object and the hitting device.

# WARM-UPS

1. The "sweet spot" for a bat or other hitting device is known in physics as the *center of oscillation* or *percussion*. It's the point where there is the least vibration (the waves of the racquet as it meets the ball are canceled out). It's easy to find it on a bat: suspend a bat by holding onto the handle; then tap the bat with a hammer, starting from the lower tip of the bat and going up. Where there's the least vibration, you'll find the "sweet spot." The center of the bat is also easy to find: balance a sideways bat on your finger; where it balances is the center of gravity. Is the center of percussion above or below the center of gravity? Do you think the two spots could be at the same point? Why?

2. When a ball hits a racquet, the impact is called *eccentric* because the two mass centers aren't moving in the same line. Tennis players look for minimum torque because it's a twisting force that the player must resist in order to keep the ball on target. *Torque* is defined as the rotational force about the axis of rotation.

STUDENT GAME PLAN

☑ **CONTEXT:** Remember those times when you hit a ball and it really stung? Remember when it "worked" and the ball sailed? The latter situation was probably due to the "sweet spot," when your movement and the vibrations of the hitting instrument (racquet or bat) canceled each other out, and the ball's energy could be used to fly to the far reaches.

☑ **CHALLENGE:** Find out what makes for an optimal hitting instrument. Does it help if it's lighter or heavier, if the handle is longer, or if you add weights or tighten strings? (And what do professional organizations have to say about changing equipment parameters?)

☑ **TASKS:**

1. Choose a sport that involves hitting an object.
2. Research the mathematical components that optimize hits.
3. Hypothesize changes in equipment that would optimize hitting.
4. Draw a diagram of the hitting instant and the forces involved; include credible mathematical quantities for the interactions.
5. Describe (by diagram, mathematical formula, model) the construction of the ideal hitting instrument.

☑ **RESOURCES:** Sources of information on sports equipment and related physics; Interactive Physics software or equivalent to test hypotheses.

☑ **ASSESSMENT:** Your final project should include the visual and mathematical description of the ideal sports equipment and mathematical evidence to support its design. You will be assessed on the thoroughness and feasibility of your design and the rigor of your mathematical defense.

☑ **STRETCHERS:**

1. Compare two hitting instruments.
2. Modify equipment for competition on the moon.

DUGOUT

The search for the perfect tennis racquet continues. Some of the more original designs have included frames with liquid inside (to redistribute weight), double stringing, and little beads or worms on the string (to lessen vibration).

Marathon: The Story of a Hit

TEACHER PLAY BOOK

☑ **ACTIVITY DESCRIPTION:** Students analyze the factors that make up a peak sports performance.

☑ **SPORTS:** All

☑ **MATHEMATICAL STRAND OUTCOMES:** Students will:
- determine which mathematical concepts apply to a sports situation
- calculate the associated mathematical terms
- determine mathematically optimal conditions for sports performance
- represent data in diagram form

☑ **INFORMATION LITERACY OUTCOMES:** Students will:
- locate information on sports performance
- identify critical factors for peak performance
- transform information into multimedia form

☑ **PREREQUISITE SKILLS:**
- computational skills
- vector analysis (optional)
- authoring software experience
- collaborative work

☑ **RATIONALE FOR THE ACTIVITY:** This activity enables students to synthesize their growing knowledge about sports performance and the myriad mathematical factors involved in making a hit or otherwise performing optimally.

☑ **COACHING TIPS:** To focus students, have them brainstorm all the factors that affect playing a sport: physiological, equipment, environment. This activity can be done on several mathematical levels. Advanced students can use calculus, advanced trigonometry, and physics concepts to make a detailed picture of a sports play. Middle schoolers can draw simpler diagrams and state general correlations between factors. This activity works well with small cooperative teams, particularly if only a few students know how to use authoring software. If such programs are not available, students can draw each step on a separate sheet in storyboard fashion.

WARM-UPS

1. A baseball hit goes about 3.5 feet less distance for every 5 mph less pitch speed. If it takes .8 second to reach the batter's box, what is the speed of the ball upon impact? (Remember: speed = distance divided by time, and the side of a baseball diamond is 90 feet long.)

2. A star batter's ball can reach a speed of 75 mph. What factors make that happen?

3. If the pitch comes in at -10° and the maximum distance is attained by hitting the ball at 25° (with the ball taking off at 125 mph from the bat), what should be its terminal distance? What is its maximum height?

STUDENT GAME PLAN

☑ **CONTEXT:** You just get up to the mound, hit the ball, and run. Right? Actually, that little scenario is a mathematical microcosm. The player's physiology and actions, the ball and bat, the other players, the stadium, and even the weather all play a role in hitting a home run.

☑ **CHALLENGE:** Get your high-speed mathematical camera out and conduct a thorough analysis of a play in sports: a bowling strike, a perfect 10 in a gymnastic routine, a goal, or a perfect serve.

☑ **TASKS:**

1. Choose a sport.
2. Determine the steps and critical features of the play: from the player's condition through the entire action and the accompanying factors.
3. For each step, determine the mathematical concepts involved.
4. Research the optimum conditions of each step and feasible mathematical values at each point.
5. Diagram each step, showing the relevant forces and functions, and calculate corresponding numerical quantities.
6. Develop a multimedia presentation of the play, step by step.

☑ **RESOURCES:** Sources of information about sports, physics, physiology, and mathematics; authoring software or storyboard supplies.

☑ **ASSESSMENT:** Your final project should consist of a step-by-step multimedia presentation of a peak sports play. You will be assessed on the mathematical rigor of your description and on the appearance and thoroughness of your diagrams.

DUGOUT

At the point of contact, a ball-bat collision can generate 10,000 pounds of force. Ouch!

Part V

Playing the Odds

Record Breaking

TEACHER PLAY BOOK

☑ **ACTIVITY DESCRIPTION:** Students track sports record-breaking achievements.

☑ **SPORTS:** All

☑ **MATHEMATICAL STRAND OUTCOMES:** Students will:
- graph discrete data
- derive functions from data (optional)
- identify dependent and independent variables
- compare graphic data mathematically
- use statistical methods to make predictions (optional)
- make predictions from graphic data

☑ **INFORMATION LITERACY OUTCOMES:** Students will:
- locate information on sports records
- determine critical features of data
- sequence information

☑ **PREREQUISITE SKILLS:**
- interpreting data in chart form
- basic graphing skills
- collaborative work

☑ **RATIONALE FOR THE ACTIVITY:** This activity enables students to get a historical perspective on sports and make reasoned predictions about future athletes. Having an interest in sports makes it easier for students to determine related data, and the two sets of data are analyzed more easily by graphing them.

☑ **COACHING TIPS:** Students may need help in breaking out two sets of data; have them brainstorm variables (e.g., gender, professional vs. amateur, different leagues, nations, etc.). Have students work in pairs, each one plotting a set of data. The task of determining the graphic format should strengthen their math knowledge. More mathematically sophisticated students can use regression analysis to make predictions or correlation coefficient calculations to test other hypotheses about the data.

WARM-UPS

1. 1998 was a record-breaking year for baseball records. Mark McGwire hit 70 home runs. If the same percentages were to apply (because there was the same number of games), and Roger Maris was at 50 at this point in time (with a season total of 61), what would be McGwire's predicted total?

2. Looking at rookie home runs gives an indication of the caliber of new baseball hires. Here are the rookies who hit more than 30 home runs by year (Sugar 1990, 30):

49	McGwire, 1987	38	Berger, 1930	38	Robinson, 1956
37	Rosen, 1950	35	Trosky, 1934	35	York, 1937
35	Dropo, 1950	33	Hall, 1963	33	Williams, 1971
32	Oliva, 1964	31	Williams, 1939	31	Hart, 1964

   Produce a scatterplot of these figures (number vs. year) and draw conclusions.

STUDENT GAME PLAN

☑ **CONTEXT:** Are athletes getting better? In 1954, the world was panting as Roger Bannister tried to run the mile in 4 minutes. Many thought that speed was impossible for humans; there was a limit to human achievement. In 1997, Algerian Moureddine Morceli ran the mile in 3:44:39 (women have yet to break the 4-minute barrier).

☑ **CHALLENGE:** Trace the history of record-breaking sports events and make predictions based on the data. Decide if there's a limit to human sports achievement.

☑ **TASKS:**

1. Choose a sport.
2. Determine a variable by which to compare two sets of records data.
3. Research your sport's record-breaking history.
4. Represent the two sets of data on one graph.
5. If possible, derive a correlation coefficient to describe the patterns in the data.
6. Analyze the data and make predictions about them.

☑ **RESOURCES:** Sources of information on sports records; graphing software, graphing calculator, or graphing supplies.

☑ **ASSESSMENT:** Your final project should consist of a graph of the two sets of data, a mathematical function to describe the trends, and an analysis of the data including predictions for future records. You will be assessed on the accuracy of your graph and function and on the mathematical rigor of your analysis and predictions.

☑ **STRETCHERS:**

1. Analyze records across sports by country.
2. Analyze records across sports for females.

DUGOUT

How many times has McGwire been walked? How many times was Babe Ruth walked?

McGwire, 146; Ruth, 170. Note: the value of a McGwire baseball card is $135, of a Maris card $425, and of a Ruth card $6,000 (Time, Sept. 14, 1998, 22).

Not all records are created equal. Although Nolan Ryan's strikeout career has lasted only 5 years, Nap Lajoie's seasonable batting average has lasted 97 years (as of 1998).

Battle of the Sexes

TEACHER PLAY BOOK

☑ **ACTIVITY DESCRIPTION:** Students compare media coverage for male and female sports.

☑ **SPORTS:** All with both male and female teams

☑ **MATHEMATICAL STRAND OUTCOMES:** Students will:
- describe sports media coverage mathematically
- determine significant differences statistically

☑ **INFORMATION LITERACY OUTCOMES:** Students will:
- locate information about sports coverage in a variety of formats
- classify information
- use content analysis to interpret data

☑ **PREREQUISITE SKILLS:**
- basic computational skills
- collaborative work

☑ **RATIONALE FOR THE ACTIVITY:** Students may spend hours reading the newspaper sports statistics pages or following ESPN coverage. However, they may not think about the quantity of coverage, although some girls are starting to notice. This activity uses mathematical content analysis to make reasonable comparisons and draw conclusions.

☑ **COACHING TIPS:** Begin the activity by having students discuss media coverage of sports. Encourage them to compare different formats (e.g., local and national newspapers, magazines, TV, radio, Internet). To introduce the idea of content analysis, have them go through their school yearbook to calculate sports coverage (and other pages of information). Have them brainstorm criteria to use in quantifying coverage: length of copy, picture size and color, placement (leading story vs. short inside clip), status of commentator, etc. To simplify the activity, have the class as a whole design the spreadsheet format (although different media typically use different criteria for judging coverage). This activity works well as a jigsaw. Have teams compare male and female coverage for one medium, then have them regroup by sport to further analyze the data. More mathematically sophisticated students can use advanced statistical methods. Less mathematically sophisticated students may use a more qualitative approach.

WARM-UPS

1. Take today's newspaper and measure the number of column inches devoted to each sport. What can you conclude?

2. Using a magazine index or an Internet search engine, count the articles or files covering each sport. What can you conclude?

STUDENT GAME PLAN

☑ **CONTEXT:** Remember looking at your school yearbook? What was the main sport covered? What about the rest of the sports? In some schools, there's more coverage of the homecoming queen than of all girls' sports. Considering the number of females in sports, are they getting their fair share of fame and glory?

☑ **CHALLENGE:** Check up on the media. Compare sports coverage for males and females using content analysis.

☑ **TASKS:**
1. As a team, choose a medium.
2. Determine how to analyze the medium's content.
3. Develop a spreadsheet template to represent the data.
4. Analyze the coverage across sports. Each team member can concentrate on one sport.
5. Statistically describe the relative amount of coverage.
6. In new teams (composed of one representative from each of the original teams), statistically analyze the data for one sport each.

☑ **RESOURCES:** Sources of information on sports coverage from a variety of formats; statistical or spreadsheet software; programmable calculators (optional).

☑ **ASSESSMENT:** Your final project should consist of two parts: a medium spreadsheet and statistical analysis, and a sports spreadsheet and statistical analysis.

☑ **STRETCHERS:**
1. Analyze sports coverage differences by team.
2. Analyze sports coverage differences by local vs. national media.
3. Analyze sports coverage differences across sports.
4. Analyze sports coverage differences according to the team's winning record.
5. Analyze sports coverage differences over time.

DUGOUT

In 1972, when Title IX was passed, 300,000 girls participated in interscholastic sports; in 1997, 2.4 million girls participated. In 1972, 90% of women's sports teams were coached by women; in 1996, only 47.7% were.

In the 1992 Winter Olympics, the United States won five gold medals. What was unique about this record?

All were won by women.

Playing Against Yourself

TEACHER PLAY BOOK

☑ **ACTIVITY DESCRIPTION:** Students analyze individual sports performance.

☑ **SPORTS:** All

☑ **MATHEMATICAL STRAND OUTCOMES:** Students will:
- represent data in graphic form
- statistically analyze data
- make predictions based on data analysis

☑ **INFORMATION LITERACY OUTCOMES:** Students will:
- locate statistical information about individual sports performance
- interpret information in chart format

☑ **PREREQUISITE SKILLS:**
- basic graphing skills
- basic statistical skills
- collaborative work

☑ **RATIONALE FOR THE ACTIVITY:** As students grow, they need to know that progress is achieved over time and is often not a linear process. This activity helps students to see the long-term changes in sports performance and to determine if there are statistical patterns in a sports career or across sports.

☑ **COACHING TIPS:** Finding career-long statistics can be challenging; more contemporary figures are usually easier to follow. As students start to trace their athletes' careers, they need to determine which statistics to follow; encourage them to include at least two different measures. This enriches the activity because students can then compare differences within one person's career. This activity works well as a jigsaw. Student pairs or triads can trace individual sports careers. In a subsequent team, they analyze data across sports.

WARM-UPS

1. A golfer tries to predict the probability that his partner will break 80. For the past 25 rounds at a par-4 hole, the partner's scores are: 4 birdies (3 strokes), 5 par (4 strokes), 6 bogies (5 strokes), 4 double bogies (6 strokes), and the rest triple bogies (7 strokes). What are the chances that the partner will shoot a par on that hole?

    a. If the other holes are of about the same difficulty, what are the chances that the partner will break 80?

    b. To be reasonably sure that the partner will break 80 twice, how many games would he have to play?

2. Would Babe Ruth have played as well now? One of the factors that has changed over the years is the quality of the entire league of baseball players. For example, when Ty Cobb was in his prime (1911 when he hit .420), he was 2.372 standard deviations above the league average of .293 and its standard deviation of 0.0326. Remembering that standard deviation equals the sum of the deviations of numbers from a mean, squared, divided by the total amount of numbers, what conclusions can you make from the following table?

Player	Batting Average	Mean Batting Average	Standard Deviation	N (# OF SD)
Lajoie (1901)	.422	.209	.0336	3.934
Boggs (1985)	.368	.268	.0264	3.808
Carew (1977)	.388	.272	.0312	3.710
Cobb (1910)	.385	.262	.0337	3.656
Williams (1941)	.406	.282	.0340	3.648

STUDENT GAME PLAN

- ☑ **CONTEXT:** Mark McGwire had the highest number of home runs for a rookie year, so it is not surprising that he became the top seasonal home run hitter. Some players last a long time: Nick Altrock played professional baseball in five decades: 1889–1933, and some gymnasts may compete for less than ten years. Some athletes start great and fizzle, while others take their time getting into top form. Some people say that each person has three peak years, then they slump. Well, it's time to set the records straight.

- ☑ **CHALLENGE:** Trace the career of a sports athlete and analyze careers within and across sports.

- ☑ **TASKS:**
    1. With one or two other students, choose a sport.
    2. Determine which attributes (e.g., speed, scores, home runs, etc.) to follow.
    3. Each person chooses one athlete to trace.
    4. Represent data in graph form.
    5. Statistically analyze individual careers longitudinally and across attributes.
    6. Graph and statistically analyze careers across athletes.
    7. Form new teams of cross-sport athletes.
    8. Graph and statistically analyze careers across sports.

- ☑ **RESOURCES:** Sources of information on athletic careers; statistics or spreadsheet software (optional); graphing software or calculators (optional).

- ☑ **ASSESSMENT:** Your final project should include three parts: a graph and statistical analysis of individual careers, a graph and statistical analysis of athletes in one sport, and a graph and statistical analysis of athletes across sports. You will be assessed on the accuracy and thoroughness of your graphs and analyses as well as on the process for designing the analyses.

- ☑ **STRETCHERS:**
    1. Compare athletes from two historical eras.
    2. Increase the number of achievement variables (e.g., home runs, RBIs, errors, etc.) and use more sophisticated statistical techniques to analyze the data.
    3. Analyze team achievement over time.

DUGOUT

During 13 years with the Chicago Bears, Walter Payton set or tied eight major NFL (National Football League) records. How many carries did he average per season?

295, a total of 3,838.

Kill the Umpire

TEACHER PLAY BOOK

- **ACTIVITY DESCRIPTION:** Students calculate the significance of officiators.

- **SPORTS:** All sports with officiators

- **MATHEMATICAL STRAND OUTCOMES:** Students will:
  - determine whether officiators are statistically biased
  - state and test null hypotheses
  - represent data in table form

- **INFORMATION LITERACY OUTCOMES:** Students will:
  - locate information about sports officiators and performance
  - interpret tabular data

- **PREREQUISITE SKILLS:**
  - distinguishing between fact and opinion
  - basic statistical skills

- **RATIONALE FOR THE ACTIVITY:** This activity helps students distinguish between possible bias and statistically random assessments.

- **COACHING TIPS:** Begin the activity by having students discuss the possible influence of biased judgment calls by officiators: umpires, referees, and judges. Point out the limitations of samples and conclusions based on insufficient evidence. To simplify the activity, have the entire class examine Olympics officiators by country.

WARM-UPS

1. Michelle Kwan easily won the 1998 Ladies World Figure Skating Championships, but some of the mid-range winners were not so unanimously determined. Here are some of the statistics:

Name/Nation	Place	Hungary	Ukraine	Sweden	Japan	Italy	Austria	Switzerland	Canada	Czech Republic
Kwiatkowski USA	6	9	6	7	4	5	9	5	4	6
Liashenko Ukraine	7	6	10	6	7	7	5	9	8	7
Sokolova Russia	8	11	9	13	8	8	7	12	14	9
Poth Hungary	9	13	16	10	10	10	10	10	10	11
Szewczenko Germany	10	8	11	12	9	9	12	7	12	10
Vorobieva Azerbaijan	11	18	8	9	11	11	6	13	11	8
Carter Austria	12	17	12	8	14	12	16	8	7	15

What statistical inferences can you make?

STUDENT GAME PLAN

☑ **CONTEXT:** "Kill the umpire!" "If the referee hadn't carded that soccer player, his team would have won the World Cup. He's prejudiced." "Well, you have to expect that the judges would go easy on their country's skater." Does a judgment call make all that much difference in determining the winner of a game?

☑ **CHALLENGE:** You be the judge. Look at assessment records and determine whether individual calls have a statistically significant "swing" effect on competition outcomes.

☑ **TASKS:**

1. Choose a sport that uses referees or judges.
2. Research their assessments and the outcomes of those competitions.
3. Represent data in table form.
4. Form a null hypothesis and alternative hypothesis about the data.
5. Statistically calculate the extent to which the assessment differences were significantly different.

☑ **RESOURCES:** Data on officiators and sports competitions; statistical software packages or programmable calculators (optional); spreadsheet software (optional).

☑ **ASSESSMENT:** Your final project should consist of a data table, working hypotheses, statistics, and conclusions. You will be assessed on the accuracy and thoroughness of your data, the appearance of your table, and the mathematical rigor of your statistics and conclusions.

☑ **STRETCHERS:**

1. Statistically compare officiators across sports.
2. Statistically compare officiators over time.

DUGOUT

The greatest number of penalties in a professional hockey game was between the Boston Bruins and the Minnesota North Stars on February 26, 1981: 406 total penalty minutes (195 for the Bruins and 211 for the North Stars).

Timing Is Everything

TEACHER PLAY BOOK

☑ **ACTIVITY DESCRIPTION:** Students analyze sports performance in relationship to timing.

☑ **SPORTS:** Those that involve timing

☑ **MATHEMATICAL STRAND OUTCOMES:** Students will:
- trace mathematically significant sports performance during a competition
- represent data in graph form
- draw conclusions from data

☑ **INFORMATION LITERACY OUTCOMES:** Students will:
- locate information on sports performance during a competition
- determine critical factors in sports performance

☑ **PREREQUISITE SKILLS:**
- basic graphing skills
- collaborative work

☑ **RATIONALE FOR THE ACTIVITY:** Sports competitions involve timing and pacing. This activity examines the scoring patterns relative to time and helps students find possible statistical correlations between the two.

☑ **COACHING TIPS:** Begin the activity by having students discuss last-minute game wins. Ask them if they think that sports teams (or individuals) wait for the final play to give their all. This activity works well as a jigsaw. The first team analyzes time patterns within a sport. New teams (composed of one representative of each original team) analyze scoring patterns between sports.

WARM-UPS

1. Assume that a team would score about the same number of points in each quarter of a game. Using the following data, determine the statistical significance of these soccer score totals relative to the quarter for 10 games:

1st Quarter	2nd Quarter	3rd Quarter	4th Quarter
2	8	4	11

2. What are the chances that a baseball World Series would last seven games? Ideally, the two teams should be equally matched. There are four possibilities: 4–0, 4–1, 4–2, 4–3. Draw a chart of the possible outcomes and calculate the odds.

   a. In actuality, baseball odds have been 4–0, 17%; 4–1, 23%; 4–2, 22%; 4–3, 38%. Are these differences statistically significant?

STUDENT GAME PLAN

☑ **CONTEXT:** Notice how often the winning touchdown is made in the last three minutes? Is this a fluke or a statistically significant occurrence? Only the mathematician knows.

☑ **CHALLENGE:** Examine the scoring patterns of sports competitions and determine whether the winning factor is time-sensitive.

☑ **TASKS:**
1. Choose a sport that is sensitive to last-minute performance. Each member chooses a different team to follow.
2. Research scores relative to time.
3. Represent scores vs. time in graphical form.
4. Draw conclusions based on the data.
5. In new student teams, compare score timing between sports.

☑ **RESOURCES:** Sources of information on scoring patterns; graphing software or calculators (optional) or graphing supplies.

☑ **ASSESSMENT:** Your final project should include a graph and analysis of one sport, and a graph and analysis between sports. You will be assessed on the accuracy and thoroughness of your graphs and on the mathematical rigor of your analysis.

☑ **STRETCHERS:**
1. Analyze scoring patterns during a season.
2. Compare amateur and professional scoring patterns.

DUGOUT

The longest professional baseball game took 25 innings; the Chicago White Sox beat the Milwaukee Brewers 7–6 on May 9, 1954. The game was tied 3–3 when the 1:00 a.m. curfew called for a next-day continuation.

A Hard Combination to Beat

TEACHER PLAY BOOK

☑ **ACTIVITY DESCRIPTION:** Students calculate sports combinations.

☑ **SPORTS:** All

☑ **MATHEMATICAL STRAND OUTCOMES:** Students will:
- identify sports combinations
- calculate sports combinations
- generate and analyze Markov chains (optional)

☑ **INFORMATION LITERACY OUTCOMES:** Students will:
- locate information about sports combinations
- diagram sports scheduling organization

☑ **PREREQUISITE SKILLS:**
- basic probability skills

☑ **RATIONALE FOR THE ACTIVITY:** A sports season gives rise to a host of combinations-related opportunities. This activity helps students realize the variety of combinations and the likelihood of specific combinations.

☑ **COACHING TIPS:** You may want to start the activity by having the class diagram an interscholastic season schedule. Markov chains can be introduced intuitively at this time. As a culminating experience, have the entire class place their sports' winning probabilities in a line, from least probable to most probable.

A Hard Combination to Beat

WARM-UPS

1. Eight students want to play pickup basketball. How many combinations are possible for choosing two teams of three each?

2. In college football, the Big Eight was renamed the Big Twelve and split into two divisions; the Western Athletic Conference (WAC) went from ten teams to four quads (divisions). If each team were to play each other team twice within their own conference or division, and then the top four were to compete in play-offs (with only winners continuing), how many games total would be played:

   a. under the Big Eight and WAC 10 setup?

   b. under the Big Twelve divisions?

   c. under the four quads?

   d. under the play-offs of the new conferences?

STUDENT GAME PLAN

☑ **CONTEXT:** Why are sports seasons getting longer? Maybe it's because more teams are playing. So what are the chances that your favorite team will be the ultimate winner? Figure it out.

☑ **CHALLENGE:** Calculate the number of games that your team will play and the chances of them becoming number one.

☑ **TASKS:**

1. Choose a sport and a team.

2. Research the number of teams, the number of divisions or conferences, and the basis for scheduling games (including play-offs). Display this information on a chart.

3. Calculate the number of games your team will play, and display the results in a Markov chain diagram.

4. Calculate the chances that they will be the ultimate winners. Revise your numbers at the critical points in the season: division win, conference win, and subsequent play-offs. Assume at each critical point that your team is eligible for the next phase.

5. Compare your team's statistics with another team's in another sport.

☑ **RESOURCES:** Sources of information on sports teams and scheduling; programmable calculator (optional).

☑ **ASSESSMENT:** Your final project should consist of a chart of your sport's scheduling organization, your team's Markov diagram, the chances of winning at each critical point, and an analysis comparing the winning chances between two sports teams. You will be assessed on the accuracy and thoroughness of your charts, the accuracy of calculated probabilities, and the mathematical rigor of your comparative analysis.

☑ **STRETCHERS:**

1. Compare chances of winning under different scheduling techniques.

2. Compare chances of winning as sports have evolved over time.

3. Calculate the chances of winning every game in a season.

DUGOUT

What are the chances of a baseball team winning the World Series after losing the first two games?

5/32 or 15.625%.

What's Your Playing Level?

TEACHER PLAY BOOK

- ☑ **ACTIVITY DESCRIPTION:** Students compare the sports performance of amateur and professional athletes.

- ☑ **SPORTS:** All

- ☑ **MATHEMATICAL STRAND OUTCOMES:** Students will:
  - calculate statistical differences between populations
  - make accurate inferences about population distribution
  - identify critical variables for population differences
  - apply analysis of variance statistical procedures (optional)
  - represent data in table form

- ☑ **INFORMATION LITERACY OUTCOMES:** Students will:
  - locate information about sports performance
  - interpret tabular information

- ☑ **PREREQUISITE SKILLS:**
  - basic statistical skills
  - ability to interpret and create data tables

- ☑ **RATIONALE FOR THE ACTIVITY:** Some students want to become professional athletes, but may not realize the differences between interscholastic and career performance. In some cases, they may attribute differences to arbitrary factors. This activity helps students make valid inferences about populations based on statistical methodology. It also emphasizes the need to look for causes for statistically valid differences.

- ☑ **COACHING TIPS:** Start the activity by having the class discuss the differences between amateur and professional sports performance. Students should consider age to be a significant variable, so when comparing two groups, it's more statistically valid to compare college or adult amateur teams with professionals rather than finding statistics of high school teams. Also discuss the statistical implications of populations and samplings. Have students brainstorm possible variables that would influence sports performance: speed, angle, power, acceleration, etc. This activity works well in pairs, one student calculating figures for amateurs and one for professionals. To simplify the activity, have students focus on individual sports or one sports position, such as goalie. Mathematically sophisticated students can use analysis of variance techniques. Statistical software and programmable calculators facilitate the calculations and help students experiment with changes in data.

# WARM-UPS

1. What distinguishes a professional team's performance from an amateur's? In examining female rowing, one possible variable is the angular velocity of the knee as the legs push back the body on the sliding seat. Using a rowing ergometer, researchers came up with these statistics (Moore and McCabe 1989, 558):

Group	Number	Mean	Standard Deviation
Amateur	10	3.02	.99
Skilled	12	4.19	.49

Assuming there is no strong skewness, state the null hypothesis (H_0) and an alternative hypothesis (H_a).

a. Are the two populations significantly different? Use a two-sample t test to determine a P-value.

b. What would be a 90% confidence interval for the difference between the knee velocities of the two populations? (*Hint:* P [lower value ≤ mean ≤ upper value] = 1 minus .1.)

124 What's Your Playing Level?

STUDENT GAME PLAN

- ☑ **CONTEXT:** Want to play golf like Tiger Woods? Watch his video! That's what the commercials say. Personal trainers say they have the answer as they analyze performance and compare it to optimum actions. But what's really valid and what's just guessing? Only the statistics can tell.

- ☑ **CHALLENGE:** Play like the pros! Find out if professional athletes really do perform quite differently from the amateurs. Then try to figure out what variable makes the difference.

- ☑ **TASKS:**
  1. In pairs, choose a sport.
  2. Research performance statistics associated with the sport: one set for amateur (such as college sports) and one set for professional.
  3. Develop a data table comparing the two sets.
  4. Statistically compare the two populations using two-sample t statistics.
  5. Determine possible variables leading to the differences and form working hypotheses.
  6. Research data related to the variables (one variable per person).
  7. Develop data tables based on the variables and test the two populations statistically.
  8. Make inferences about the two sets of sports performances.

- ☑ **RESOURCES:** Sources of information on sports performance and statistics; statistical software packages or spreadsheet software (optional); programmable calculators (optional).

- ☑ **ASSESSMENT:** Your final project should consist of two parts: data tables and statistics for the two populations, and hypotheses, data tables, and statistics for testing the performance variable. You will be assessed on the accuracy and thoroughness of your tables and statistics, the feasibility of your hypothesis, and the mathematical rigor of your process.

- ☑ **STRETCHERS:**
  1. Statistically compare performance for players in the same position across teams.
  2. Statistically compare similar actions (e.g., throwing) across sports.

DUGOUT

Babe Ruth kept his lead shoulder pointed at his target as long as possible before pulling his throwing arm through; it made him a stronger and more accurate outfielder. Why?

Playing Your Part

TEACHER PLAY BOOK

- ☑ **ACTIVITY DESCRIPTION:** Students analyze the significance of each player in a winning team.

- ☑ **SPORTS:** All team sports

- ☑ **MATHEMATICAL STRAND OUTCOMES:** Students will:
  - calculate statistical correlations between individual player performance and team wins
  - use matrices to determine winning combinations (optional)

- ☑ **INFORMATION LITERACY OUTCOMES:** Students will:
  - locate information on individual player and team achievements
  - identify critical attributes of team players

- ☑ **PREREQUISITE SKILLS:**
  - basic statistical skills

- ☑ **RATIONALE FOR THE ACTIVITY:** In the final analysis, either a team wins or loses. However, each player contributes to the final score. This activity allows students to calculate the statistical significance of individual players' performances.

- ☑ **COACHING TIPS:** More mathematically sophisticated students can use ANOVA and other multiple regression analysis. Students may also examine each position in light of the team scores.

 **WARM-UPS**

1. In 1998 it seemed that everyone focused on the batter in baseball, but the pitchers had a winning season too. As of September 6, here are the statistics for the top six (Farber 1998, 41):

Pitcher / Team	Record	% Wins
David Wells / Yankees	17–2	.895
John Smoltz / Braves	14–3	.824
Pedro Martinez / Red Sox	18–4	.818
Kevin Brown / Padres	18–5	.783
David Cone / Yankees	18–5	.783
Roger Clemens / Blue Jays	18–6	.750

What statistical inferences can you make?

   a. At the same point, the Blue Jays were 24.5 games behind the Yankees in the American League East. If Clemens wins the American League Cy Young Award (which is likely), the Blue Jays will be further from first place than all but two teams with Cy Young winners. What are the statistical implications?

2. Examine the statistics for current team competitions (look in the newspaper or on the Internet). Noting the performances of each position, what statistical inferences can you make about each player's contribution to the final scores?

   a. Examine the injury list for a sport and determine if there's a statistical significance in the team's performance.

STUDENT GAME PLAN

☑ **CONTEXT:** Who wins the game? The team. Yet people remember the individual players. Was Wayne Gretsky the key to hockey, or is some forgotten goalie the reason why the Kings had a winning season? Just because Michael Jordan was great in basketball didn't mean his baseball team would win. Just how much are team sports really a team effort?

☑ **CHALLENGE:** Calculate the individual and cumulative efforts of team players.

☑ **TASKS:**

1. In a group, choose a sport. Each member chooses a team.
2. Research the performance of individual players and team scores.
3. Produce a spreadsheet of the team results and individual performance.
4. Analyze the data for statistical significance. You might derive the correlation coefficient of the individual efforts in terms of each other and the team as a whole. You may also try a chi-square technique to determine the significance of individual efforts.
5. In the group teams (where each member has the data for professional teams within the same sport), statistically analyze the significance of individuals across teams.

☑ **RESOURCES:** Sources of information about individual and team performance; statistical or spreadsheet software (optional); programmable calculators (optional).

☑ **ASSESSMENT:** Your final project should consist of two parts: a team data spreadsheet, and statistical analysis; and a sports statistical analysis. You will be assessed on the accuracy and thoroughness of your spreadsheet and statistics and on the mathematical rigor of your sports analysis.

☑ **STRETCHERS:**

1. Statistically analyze the interaction of teams.
2. Statistically analyze teams over time.
3. Statistically analyze individual players' contributions when they change teams.

DUGOUT

Who was the only Super Bowl athlete who also played on a major league baseball team?

Tom Brown (for the Green Bay Packers and the Washington Senators).

Marathon: Dream Teams

TEACHER PLAY BOOK

☑ **ACTIVITY DESCRIPTION:** Students create dream sports teams and compete with them (in simulation) using mathematical probabilities.

☑ **SPORTS:** All team sports

☑ **MATHEMATICAL STRAND OUTCOMES:** Students will:
- calculate the relative statistical standings for athletes
- use probability to determine competition outcomes
- represent data in table form

☑ **INFORMATION LITERACY OUTCOMES:** Students will:
- locate information on sport teams
- interpret sports statistics
- develop and implement simulations

☑ **PREREQUISITE SKILLS:**
- basic statistical and probability skills
- basic sports knowledge
- practice with simulations
- collaborative work

☑ **RATIONALE FOR THE ACTIVITY:** Winning teams are a combination of statistics, probability, and luck, as well as economics. This activity enables students to synthesize their understanding of comparative statistics and the "luck of the draw."

☑ **COACHING TIPS:** Tie this activity to an all-star game, before names are announced. This timing gives students more incentive and provides professional feedback on their assessments. This activity works well with pairs developing their dream teams. They then compete with another pair (say a National League team vs. an American League team). Have the competing pairs develop the "rules" of the simulation. To simplify the activity, have students choose winners for individual sports, such as golf or dressage. You may also have students play fantasy sports on the Internet.

WARM-UPS

1. A recent fantasy football list for right drafts included these statistics:

Name	Average Rank	High Rank	Low Rank	Total	Times on Draft List
Davis	1.50	1	3	69	30
Sanders	2.30	1	6	168	30
Bettis	5.60	3	11	189	30
Levens	6.30	3	12	189	30
George	8.67	1	18	260	30
Dillon	11.13	3	27	334	30
Watters	11.17	6	23	335	30
Faulk	14.60	8	29	438	30
Kaufman	16.07	10	36	482	30

What statistical inferences can you make from this data?

a. On the overall draft list, of the top ten draftees eight were running back positions and two were quarterback positions. What might you infer from those choices?

2. The following odds were given for upcoming tennis matches:

Event	Favorite	Underdog	Points If Favorite Wins	Points If Underdog Wins
Women's US Open Finals	Hingis	Davenport	48	52
Men's US Open Semifinal 1	Sampras	Rafter	43	57
Men's US Open Semifinal 2	Moya	Philippoussis	41	59
Men's US Open Finals	Sampras or Rafter	Moya or Philippoussis	50	50

What statistical inferences can you make from this data?

# STUDENT GAME PLAN

- ☑ **CONTEXT:** Remember the Dream Team for the Olympic basketball event? Consider the all-star games. These events spotlight individual accomplishments and "up the ante" for competition. In a way, they fulfill our fantasies of matching the best with the best.

- ☑ **CHALLENGE:** Create a dream team and have them compete with another dream team in a simulation.

- ☑ **TASKS:**
    1. In pairs, choose a sport.
    2. Research the performance of relevant players.
    3. Using statistics, develop a dream team.
    4. Develop a simulation for the dream team competition.
    5. Play the simulation.

- ☑ **RESOURCES:** Sources of information on sports performance and statistics (e.g., http://www.usfantasy411.com); simulation supplies.

- ☑ **ASSESSMENT:** Your final project should consist of the dream team lineup, statistical "evidence" for the team choices, simulation setup, and results of the simulated game. You will be assessed on the mathematical rigor of your team choices, the thoroughness and logic of your simulation setup, and the mathematical rigor of your simulation.

- ☑ **STRETCHERS:**
    1. Create a historical dream team.
    2. Create a nightmare team.

DUGOUT

Name the original Olympic Basketball Dream Team members.

Charles Barkley, Larry Bird, Clyde Drexler, Patrick Ewing, Magic Johnson, Michael Jordan, Christian Laettner, Karl Malone, Chris Mullin, Scottie Pippen, David Robinson, and John Stockton.

Whom did they beat?

Croatia, 117–85.

Part VI

Sports for (Fun and) Profit

The Independent Spirit

TEACHER PLAY BOOK

- ☑ **ACTIVITY DESCRIPTION:** Students investigate the economics of individual sports.

- ☑ **SPORTS:** Individual sports, such as golf, bowling, fencing, and weight-lifting.

- ☑ **MATHEMATICAL STRAND OUTCOMES:** Students will:
  - calculate the revenue and expenditure for individual sports
  - represent data in graph and spreadsheet form

- ☑ **INFORMATION LITERACY OUTCOMES:** Students will:
  - locate information on individual sports
  - identify significant economic factors in individual sports

- ☑ **PREREQUISITE SKILLS:**
  - basic spreadsheet and graphing skills
  - collaborative work

- ☑ **RATIONALE FOR THE ACTIVITY:** Individual sports represents a different spin on expenditures and revenue: training costs, transportation, capital outlay, sponsorships, etc. This activity helps students realize the economic factors behind individual sports.

- ☑ **COACHING TIPS:** Begin the activity by having students identify sports that allow for individual competition: equestrian, tennis, track, golf, etc. Then have them brainstorm expenditures and revenues for individual sports: transportation, training, accounting, promotion, etc. Have each student research one athlete, and then compare the financial picture with other students' athletes; ideally, a couple of students would follow athletes in the same sport and then compare their financial pictures with athletes in other sports.

WARM-UPS

1. Two auto racers tied for the most victories in a season: 10. However, a different racer, Emerson Fittipaldi, garnered the highest single-season winnings: $2,166,078. If the tie-winners had won that amount in each race, what would have been their winnings per race?

    a. How do you think Fittipaldi won more money than the top racers?

2. The top woman tennis player in 1998 won $1,831,971 as of August 25; the leading man won $1,643,471. What is the percentage difference?

    a. For the top five women, the average winning for the same time period was $985,235; for the top five men it was $1,348,555. What is the percentage difference?

    b. In tenth place for women's winnings for the same time period was Patty Schnyder with $386,913; the men's counterpart was Andre Agassi at $790,018. What conclusions or issues can you raise about winnings for men and women in professional tennis?

3. In 1875 the Kentucky Derby winner received $2,850. In 1997 the purse was $700,000. What is the percentage difference?

    a. Find the price index over the years and recalculate the value of the purse.

STUDENT GAME PLAN

☑ **CONTEXT:** Teamwork is all fine and good, but can't you make more money going it alone? Think of those golf purses of a million dollars. Consider the prestige and salaries of top individual skaters. In a team sport, you're only as good as the rest of the team, so maybe going solo is the best alternative.

☑ **CHALLENGE:** Imagine yourself as a professional single. Calculate the costs for entering a major competition and the payback.

☑ **TASKS:**

1. Choose an individual sport.
2. Choose a competition in that sport.
3. Determine the costs associated with the competition.
4. Research those costs and create a spreadsheet quantifying them.
5. Calculate the relative benefits depending on the outcome: first, second, third.
6. Research the feasible endorsements related to the standings of that event (e.g., first at Wimbledon). Incorporate that information into the spreadsheet.
7. Compare your individual's financial picture with at least one other person's.

☑ **RESOURCES:** Sources of information on the economics of individual sports; spreadsheet program or supplies.

☑ **ASSESSMENT:** Your final project should consist of a spreadsheet and a comparative analysis. You will be assessed on the reasonableness of the data, the accuracy of the spreadsheet, and the logic of your analysis.

☑ **STRETCHERS:**

1. Compare the economics of individual and team sports.
2. Calculate the agent's costs relative to the player's.

DUGOUT

Though both Al Unser and Rick Mears were top money-earners for four years each, Unser earned $2,814,615 while Mears won $4,162,989. Explain the difference.

Mears's years were more recent, and the pots were different.

For the Love of the Game

TEACHER PLAY BOOK

☑ **ACTIVITY DESCRIPTION:** Students compare revenue and expenses for different levels of amateur sports teams.

☑ **SPORTS:** Amateur team sports

☑ **MATHEMATICAL STRAND OUTCOMES:** Students will:
- calculate revenue and expenses
- represent data in spreadsheet form
- make predictions by manipulating spreadsheet data
- analyze and compare data

☑ **INFORMATION LITERACY OUTCOMES:** Students will:
- locate information from a variety of sources about sport team economics
- determine critical economic factors
- interpret spreadsheet data

☑ **PREREQUISITE SKILLS:**
- basic spreadsheet skills
- collaborative work

☑ **RATIONALE FOR THE ACTIVITY:** At every level, there are expenses to manage a team. Often students don't realize that their own school athletic program can burn a hole in the academic pocket; costs may be absorbed in different budgets, but they still have to be paid somehow. This activity helps students compare team finance across sports and across amateur levels.

☑ **COACHING TIPS:** Start the activity by discussing the revenue and expenditure sources for operating an amateur team. Encourage them to interview local athletic directors and parent booster clubs. It is easier to compare figures if the whole class designs the spreadsheet structure together. This activity works well with a jigsaw structure. To simplify the activity, the class may focus on one sport, with the first round divided by type of expenditure (one student per level); the second round would then synthesize the costs within each level.

WARM-UPS

1. In order to attract funding to support their programs, the Inner City Handball Association (ICHA) offers Web site services to donors. For one month the use includes:

   - 33 listed sponsors ($100 per month for each)
   - $50 marquee advertisement
   - $300 Web site of the month
   - 18 tournament listings ($150 per year)

   Assuming that the numbers didn't change, what would be the income from ICHA's Web site?

2. A 16-team Division I college football play-off could generate $60 million, on top of the $41 million generated by the 19-bowl system for participating teams and conference members. However, the idea was killed. Why? The NCAA (National Collegiate Athletic Association) would divide the money among all the schools in three divisions: more than 800. It was said that for a conference with one or two teams playing in bowls, it was profitable; for conferences having seven such teams, there would be a financial loss. Explain.

STUDENT GAME PLAN

☑ **CONTEXT:** At any level of play, a team can cost a lot. Even Little League needs sponsors to help pay for uniforms. Public school isn't a free ride either. Even colleges have to pay out big time in the hopes of having a winning, if nonprofit, team.

☑ **CHALLENGE:** Compare team economics by level: junior league, high school varsity, collegiate, and community. Decide what level of team you would want to act as financial manager for.

☑ **TASKS:**

1. Choose a sport.
2. Choose a level; you may also decide to compare a male and a female team such as basketball.
3. Identify the sources of revenue and expenditures for the team.
4. Research representative financial figures for your type of team.
5. Create one spreadsheet for the specific team and one for the sport in general (the collaborate group's efforts).
6. Develop graphs to visually compare the teams' financial pictures.
7. With others at the same level (e.g., high school varsity) representing different sports, create a composite spreadsheet and comparative graphs.
8. Analyze the data and determine the team for which you would like to be the financial manager.

☑ **RESOURCES:** Sources of information on sports economics; spreadsheet software (or supplies).

☑ **ASSESSMENT:** Your final project should consist of three parts: team and sports spreadsheets, graphs, and analysis; a level spreadsheet, graphs, and analysis; and a financial manager analysis. You will be assessed on the feasibility of the team's economics, the accuracy and thoroughness of your data representation, and the logic of your analysis and decision making.

☑ **STRETCHERS:**

1. Compare team economics over time (e.g., difference between the 1950s and the 1990s).
2. Compare economics in sports overseas.
3. Investigate the economics of Olympic teams.
4. Compare amateur and professional sports economics.

DUGOUT

Quarterback Troy Aikman became the highest-paid NFL player in 1993 when he signed an eight-year, $50 million contract with the Dallas Cowboys.

When the 1994 baseball strike was over, the losses were estimated to be $442 million in owners' revenues and over $235 million in player salaries—and that didn't count postseason finances.

Fit for Business

TEACHER PLAY BOOK

- ☑ **ACTIVITY DESCRIPTION:** Students develop a financial plan for a fitness center.

- ☑ **SPORTS:** All associated with fitness centers

- ☑ **MATHEMATICAL STRAND OUTCOMES:** Students will:
  - identify and calculate economic factors in managing a fitness center
  - use matrices to determine business decisions (optional)
  - represent data in spreadsheet form
  - make economic predictions based on data

- ☑ **INFORMATION LITERACY OUTCOMES:** Students will:
  - locate information on fitness centers
  - interpret accounting data

- ☑ **PREREQUISITE SKILLS:**
  - basic spreadsheet skills
  - basic accounting skills
  - interviewing skills (optional)

- ☑ **RATIONALE FOR THE ACTIVITY:** Fitness centers are big business, and the idea of opening a franchise can be appealing. However, the economic details of starting and maintaining such a business can surprise the young entrepreneur. This activity provides students with economic insights into starting such endeavors. It also provides concrete accounting figures upon which students can make economic predictions and decisions.

- ☑ **COACHING TIPS:** Begin the activity by having students brainstorm the factors involved in starting and maintaining a fitness center: personnel, facilities, legalities, PR, equipment, etc. Encourage students (in pairs) to interview the staff at local fitness centers. They should have a list of interview questions before their visit and should schedule their interview ahead of time. Particularly if few such centers exist locally, students may correspond on the Internet or expand their topic by looking at community centers, school athletic programs, or nonprofit groups. This activity should be done in small cooperative teams. The easiest way to structure the plan is to have one person each studying location/facility and pricing/advertising, and two each on the start-up budget and operating budget. To simplify the activity, have the entire class research one fitness center, with half of the teams focusing on start-up costs and half on operating costs (pairs can look at one factor, such as utilities, from start-up and ongoing expense).

WARM-UPS

1. A fitness center decides to convert an underused racquetball court into a climbing wall to attract new business. They calculate about 2,200 square feet and $50 per square foot modification cost. What is the total cost for the new wall?

    a. No more than five people can be on the wall at the same time, for safety reasons. Each climber has to take a one-hour orientation class. A day pass is $10 and an orientation class is $18, which includes the daily pass fee. Assuming that no extra labor cost is involved, what kind of business (e.g., number of people and turnaround time) would it take to pay for the wall in a year if the center were open from noon to 10:00 p.m. 360 days a year? Draw a graph to show the relationship between number of people and length of time on the wall.

2. Using a weighted score is an effective way to compare products or services. Individual factors are rated 4 (excellent) to 1 (poor), and each factor is given a percentage based on its importance, with the total number equal to one. Whichever product has the highest number "wins." For example, two fitness centers may be rated as follows:

Factors	Weight	A Rating	A Score	B Rating	B Score
Service	.40	3	1.20	4	1.60
Price	.30	3	?	2	?
Convenience	.20	3	?	4	?
Safety	.10	4	?	2	?
TOTAL	1.00	–	?	–	?

Complete the chart.

STUDENT GAME PLAN

☑ **CONTEXT:** Fitness centers are big business these days. If you include school-connected and organizational centers (such as the YMCA), almost every community has one. One reason they're so popular is that people want to get into shape and stay that way. Most physical fitness trainers don't require lots of academic training, either; they tend to learn on the job. When you consider that franchises offer instant advertising, it starts to sound like a good sports business investment. So why do you see gyms and other centers going out of business? It takes more brain than brawn.

☑ **CHALLENGE:** You have $100,000 to invest in a fitness center. Develop a profitable business plan for the year.

☑ **TASKS:**

1. Research how to develop a business plan. A good start is the Web site for the Small Business Administration: http://www.sba.gov.
2. Identify start-up and operating costs. Research reasonable data for each.
3. Develop a start-up budget and a monthly operating budget.
4. Determine the revenue sources for the business and develop reasonable data for them.
5. Develop a monthly revenue plan.
6. Create a monthly spreadsheet ledger showing revenue and expenditures for the first year of the business.

☑ **RESOURCES:** Sources of information on fitness centers, accounting, and business ventures; spreadsheet program or supplies.

☑ **ASSESSMENT:** Your final project should consist of a year-long business plan, including supporting data in spreadsheet form and logical arguments for the plan. You will be assessed on the feasibility of your plan, the accuracy and thoroughness of your data, and the logic of your decision making.

☑ **STRETCHERS:**

1. Investigate the cost of developing or maintaining a professional sports facility.
2. Compare the cost of starting a business "from scratch" or buying a franchise.

DUGOUT

There are 2,227 YMCAs serving 16 million people; it's the nation's largest nonprofit community service organization.

Cities and Franchises: A Marriage Made in Heaven?

TEACHER PLAY BOOK

☑ **ACTIVITY DESCRIPTION:** Students analyze the economic impact of sports franchises.

☑ **SPORTS:** Professional sports franchises

☑ **MATHEMATICAL STRAND OUTCOMES:** Students will:
- develop a cost analysis of a sports franchise and city economics
- represent data in presentation form
- make economic predictions based on data analysis
- use regression analysis to determine relative impact of factors (optional)
- make persuasive arguments based on the data

☑ **INFORMATION LITERACY OUTCOMES:** Students will:
- locate information on sports franchises and city economics
- identify economic factors associated with sports franchises
- determine bias in information

☑ **PREREQUISITE SKILLS:**
- basic spreadsheet skills (optional)
- collaborative work

☑ **RATIONALE FOR THE ACTIVITY:** Sports teams are big business these days, and owners now scout out the best financial deals for their teams. Cities, too, are looking for new revenue. However, both sides must seriously invest in order to reap the benefits. In some cases, it's a win-win situation; in others, both may lose. This activity helps students realize the many factors that influence sports and urban economics—and the difference that perspective makes in analyzing and manipulating data.

☑ **COACHING TIPS:** To focus the class, have them develop a list of economic factors affecting sports franchises and another list of factors for urban financial well-being. As students research the problem, they will find new factors, which they can add to the two class lists. This activity works most easily in cooperative teams of four: two representing the sports managers and two representing urban interests. A more complex way to structure this activity is to have students list different constituents (e.g., team manager, team owner, team members, stadium director, mayor, concessionaires, transportation managers, local employment service, neighborhood families, police, sports fans) who would be affected by the franchise and conduct a panel discussion. Although ideally, each team selects a different city and team to research the actual economics involved, students may also construct imaginary yet feasible scenarios. To encourage diversity, have each panel choose a different sport. Also encourage students to think in the long term as well as the short term. It's fun to have an outside expert decide the issue based on the evidence. Discuss ways to present data in a compelling way (this is a good opportunity to show how statistics can be manipulated).

WARM-UPS

1. The average football ticket in 1991 cost about $25; in 1997 it was about $38. The average 1991 player salary was $157,000; in 1998, $751,000. The average game attendance in 1991 was about 60,000; in 1997, 62,500. All other factors being equal, what is the percentage difference in profits for football owners?

2. Already $24 billion has been allocated for building sports facilities by 2005, and 75 to 80% of the money will come from the public — most from tax-free bonds. Because of this, the federal government loses out on an average of 4% on construction costs. How much less revenue will the government receive because of these commitments?

3. To pay for NFL broadcasting rights, Fox is demanding that local stations pay at least $30 million of the cost. In turn, the stations charge more for local advertising. Assuming that the football season is 16 weeks long, that Fox broadcasts two games weekly, that they show the 12 play-offs, and that they have 176 affiliate stations, how much advertising revenue would they have to get per game (assuming that stations can charge twice as much during play-offs) (McGraw 1998, 40–46)?

    a. Make a chart that shows the rate as a function of the number of ads per game.

STUDENT GAME PLAN

- ☑ **CONTEXT:** You hear that your favorite football team wants to come to your city. "Great news!" you think. It'll open up more jobs, maybe one for you, and you can finally go to their games even if they don't hire you. By the way, the owners want a new stadium; they'll even pay for half of it. Is that a good thing? What impact does a sports franchise have on the local economy? To a degree, it depends on your perspective. Traditionally, having a local sports team benefited a city, but recent studies show that the picture isn't so rosy. It's your call.

- ☑ **CHALLENGE:** It's a "town hall" meeting in your city to decide whether to permit a team to move to your locale. Constituents affected by the decision come to present their cases using mathematical evidence. May the best "team" win.

- ☑ **TASKS:**
    1. Create a panel of pro-franchise and anti-franchise constituents.
    2. Identify a city and a sports team/franchise.
    3. Research economic factors related to the problem.
    4. Analyzing the data mathematically, develop arguments and evidence to support your stance.
    5. Represent your data in a compelling form.
    6. Convince the class (or other decision maker) of your point of view, based on your mathematical argument.

- ☑ **RESOURCES:** Sources of information on sports economics, urban demographics, and finances; spreadsheet software (optional); presentation software or supplies.

- ☑ **ASSESSMENT:** Your final project should consist of your presentation and data documentation. You will be assessed on the persuasiveness of your evidence.

- ☑ **STRETCHERS:**
    1. Calculate one to ten years ahead in presenting the case for a sports franchise.
    2. Research the history of sports franchises and their effect on the local economy.

DUGOUT

Washington taxpayers voted for a $300 million bond to pay for a new stadium for the Seattle Seahawks, owned by billionaire and Microsoft cofounder Paul Allen. A statewide referendum soon followed.

It Takes a Village to Put on a Sports Event

TEACHER PLAY BOOK

☑ **ACTIVITY DESCRIPTION:** Students explore the labor expenses related to a sports event.

☑ **SPORTS:** All

☑ **MATHEMATICAL STRAND OUTCOMES:** Students will:
- calculate labor costs related to a sports event
- represent data in sociogram and graphic form
- compare economic data

☑ **INFORMATION LITERACY OUTCOMES:** Students will:
- locate information on sports events
- determine labor factors and relationships in a sports event

☑ **PREREQUISITE SKILLS:**
- basic spreadsheet skills
- basic calculation skills
- ability to draw a sociogram
- collaborative work

☑ **RATIONALE FOR THE ACTIVITY:** When we watch the Super Bowl, we see the pageantry and hear about the player bonuses. But the behind-the-scenes work—and payoffs—make the high-profile event possible. This activity helps students realize the interdependent nature of sports event planning and follow-through. They can also use this information to see the broader economic picture and explore sports-related careers.

☑ **COACHING TIPS:** Start the activity by having students generate a list of sports events. Then have them list all the possible people involved in putting on that event. Students may want to interview stadium/fairground event planners. Students may need help in drawing sociograms. This activity works well in small cooperative teams. To extend the activity, pairs of teams compare the financial and personnel implications of a sports event.

WARM-UPS

1. Every year Denmark hosts the Dana Cup, an international soccer tournament for youth players. About 20,000 participate, and each player may have free transportation from the airport to the local lodging as well as from their lodging to the playing field. If the average cost for a taxi ride is $30 and a one-way bus trip is $1.25, how much money must be found to underwrite the transportation cost? Hertz was willing to foot the taxi bill. If their normal profit is 25%, what is their in-kind contribution in dollars?

2. For the 1999 Special Olympics in North Carolina 35,000 volunteers were needed; 7,000 athletes from 150 countries competed in 19 sports. On average, how many volunteers is that per participant and per sport?

3. The Nagano Olympic Organizing Committee for the 1998 Winter Olympics consisted of 158 prefectural civil servants, 72 Nagano City civil servants, 104 people from national governing bodies, 197 people from private industry, and 96 committee employees and temporary staff. How many staff members were there in total?

   a. Draw a pie chart of the committee constituents and calculate the relative percentage of each group. What percentage were government related?

148 It Takes a Village to Put on a Sports Event

☑ **CONTEXT:** You hear about the million-dollar bonuses for Super Bowl players, and think these guys are the heart of the event. Then you remember the million dollars spent in advertisement spots. Plus, there's the camera crew, announcers, standby ambulance, ticketers, concession stands, stadium managers, and so on. If the same teams were playing on a vacant lot with no one around, would they get those fancy rings? Nope. Although it's hard to put a price tag on people, it would be misleading not to take into account their contributions to a sports event.

☑ **CHALLENGE:** Create a financial sociogram of a sports event. What is each entity's contribution and how are they compensated financially?

☑ **TASKS:**

1. Identify a sports event.
2. Identify the key people or entities that make the event happen.
3. Find out the financial implication of their involvement.
4. As needed, research which people are needed to support the key personnel and their financial impact.
5. Draw a sociogram of the people involved in the sports event, attaching financial figures to them. You may want to draw a bar graph for each, comparing the income and outgo for each entity.
6. Create a pie chart to represent each entity's financial contribution and benefit.

☑ **RESOURCES:** Sources of information on sports events and sports-related careers; spreadsheet and bar graph programs or supplies.

☑ **ASSESSMENT:** Your final project should consist of a sociogram and an analysis of the data. You will be assessed on the accuracy and thoroughness of your sociogram and charts as well as on the logic of your analysis.

☑ **STRETCHERS:**

1. Trace the financial distribution of a year's worth of events at a stadium.
2. Compare the financial implications of two different sports events.

 **DUGOUT**

Does drama pay? The 1994 Olympics women's skating short program (featuring dueling Tonya Harding and Nancy Kerrigan) rated a 64% share of viewers: 12.6 million.

It Pays to Win

TEACHER PLAY BOOK

☑ **ACTIVITY DESCRIPTION:** Students investigate the financial implications of winning teams.

☑ **SPORTS:** Team sports

☑ **MATHEMATICAL STRAND OUTCOMES:** Students will:
- calculate economic factors for teams
- determine the statistical significance for sports team finances
- represent data in spreadsheet or graphic form
- make predictions based on the data

☑ **INFORMATION LITERACY OUTCOMES:** Students will:
- locate information on sports teams
- interpret numerical data

☑ **PREREQUISITE SKILLS:**
- basic calculation skills
- basic statistical skills
- collaborative work

☑ **RATIONALE FOR THE ACTIVITY:** What's the best indicator of a team sports financial picture? Winning! Students have an opportunity to test this assertion by calculating the benefits of play-offs and winning teams.

☑ **COACHING TIPS:** Start the activity by having students brainstorm the benefits of winning teams: play-offs, game attendance, endorsements, etc. This activity works well in pairs in which each person researches the data for his or her team and then compares the results.

WARM-UPS

1. Professional football teams received more than $49 million in radio payments for broadcast rights in 1992. That same year, baseball received about $13 million. What is the percentage difference between the two sports? If you know the number of games per season, what is the differential taking that into account?

2. The NFL caps salaries at 64% of league revenues. If that's $34.6 million per team (14 teams), what were the total league revenues?

    a. A four-team NFL play-off is worth about $100 million in revenues. How much is that per game, per team, and per player if all are counted equally?

STUDENT GAME PLAN

- ☑ **CONTEXT:** What's the best predictor of financial success for a team? A prepaid stadium, cheap players, a low standard of living? It's having a winning team. Why? Because they play longer (through the play-offs) and attract bigger crowds. Think of some other reasons.

- ☑ **CHALLENGE:** Trace the financial benefits accorded to winning teams and the impact on losing teams. You will be seeking financial backing for a team, based on the data.

- ☑ **TASKS:**
    1. Choose a sport.
    2. Identify possible financial factors that would influence team profitability.
    3. Identify a winning team and a losing team in the same sport.
    4. Trace the various factors that could differentiate the two teams.
    5. Develop statistical hypotheses and test them in terms of team profitability.
    6. Represent the data in visual form and present it.

- ☑ **RESOURCES:** Sources of information on sports teams; statistical packages (optional); data representation programs or supplies.

- ☑ **ASSESSMENT:** Your final project should consist of comparative figures for the two teams, statistical visuals, and an explanation of the teams' profitability. You will be assessed on the accuracy and thoroughness of your data and its representation and on the mathematical rigor of your argument.

- ☑ **STRETCHERS:**
    1. Compare the benefits of winning teams across sports.
    2. Investigate the betting situation relative to sports teams.

DUGOUT

In 1992 the Los Angeles Lakers pulled in $19.3 million from TV contracts alone.

It's All in the Cards

TEACHER PLAY BOOK

☑ **ACTIVITY DESCRIPTION:** Students investigate the economics of sports card collecting.

☑ **SPORTS:** Those having cards (e.g., baseball, football, Olympics)

☑ **MATHEMATICAL STRAND OUTCOMES:** Students will:
- use statistics and probability to analyze data
- represent data in graphic and spreadsheet form
- make predictions based on data analysis

☑ **INFORMATION LITERACY OUTCOMES:** Students will:
- locate information on sports card collecting
- identify economic factors in sports card collecting

☑ **PREREQUISITE SKILLS:**
- basic graphing skills
- basic statistical and probability skills
- knowledge of economic principles
- collaborative work

☑ **RATIONALE FOR THE ACTIVITY:** Most young people like to collect things; sports cards can be a fun and profitable venture — maybe even a career. This activity shows the complex background of card collecting and helps students understand economic principles through spreadsheets and supply-demand curves.

☑ **COACHING TIPS:** Start the activity by having students brainstorm factors to be considered when starting a business: production and packaging, marketing and selling, copyright fees, photography, writing and editing labor, mailing and distribution, facilities (for manufacturing, exhibiting, and selling), taxes (for materials, property, and capital gains), and optional stock distribution. Next, have students generate a list of economic issues, such as the quantity needed to make a profit, ways to lower expenses, and the impact of advertising. To simplify the activity, have students focus on one or two variables, such as comparing two production alternatives or two selling methods (mail order vs. store outlets). This activity works well in small collaborative teams; each member can focus on a different aspect of the business: production, design, promotion, or accounting.

WARM-UPS

1. In 1985 the baseball card market accounted for $46 million in sales. In 1986 it grew to $81 million, and by 1990 it was $325 million. If the market continues to grow at the same rate, by what year will the sports card business hit the billion-dollar mark?

2. In one year a company shipped 270,054 cases of baseball cards. Of these, 160,728 (1.74 billion cards) were sold in foil packs; 62,266 cases (747.2 million cards) were sold in complete sets; 24,726 cases (213.6 million cards) were sold in grocery store display units; and 15,313 cases (147 million cards) were sold as singles (Williams 1995, 145). How many cards were in each case by type of sales?

    a. Create two pie charts (one by number of cases, one by number of actual cards) to show the distribution pattern.

3. At one point, baseball players were paid $125 each for the right of a card manufacturer to use their pictures for the whole year; that company made millions from the sale of baseball cards. The baseball union was upset and made a new deal in 1968: manufacturers paid each player $250, royalties of 8% on sales up to $4 million, and royalties of 10% for sales beyond that figure. That year, union players received $320,000 in royalties for $4 million worth of sales (Williams 1995, 25–28). If a company usually produced an 80-card series, how much did each player make altogether in 1968 if each one was paid the same amount?

    a. How much did the manufacturer have to pay in total, and how much was profit (not counting other expenses)?

STUDENT GAME PLAN

- ☑ **CONTEXT:** Do you think collecting sports cards is just a kid's pastime? At one point, Mickey Mantle made $2.75 million signing sports memorabilia. The rarest baseball card, T206 Horace Wagner in 1909, was sold in 1996 for $640,000 (it was originally a free premium with a tobacco purchase). It's all in how you play your cards.

- ☑ **CHALLENGE:** Imagine that you are starting a business producing and trading sports cards. Factor in the various expenses and develop a business plan for a formal presentation.

- ☑ **TASKS:**
    1. Decide what kind of card business to start.
    2. Determine the factors needed to operate the business.
    3. Research the cost for each factor. You may want to interview card deals, read trade magazines, and examine other production and sales business.
    4. Develop a spreadsheet to show the different factors. Structure it by calculating the revenue and expenses in terms of a card's unit price.
    5. Research economic relationships, such as profit/expenses and supply/demand. Show how they apply to your business by representing the data in graphic form (e.g., unit cost of production in lots of hundreds, thousands, millions).
    6. Using the spreadsheet to make predictions, explore at least two alternative business plans.
    7. Develop a business plan presentation in mathematical terms.

- ☑ **RESOURCES:** Sources of information on card collecting (a good start is Williams's *Card Sharks*, 1995); catalogs of card collections; entrepreneurs in card collecting.

- ☑ **ASSESSMENT:** Your final project should consist of a business plan presentation that incorporates the spreadsheets and graphs. You will be assessed on the feasibility of your plan, the accuracy and thoroughness of your data representations, and your step-by-step assumptions and decisions.

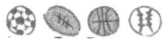

☑ STRETCHERS:

1. Compare the cost of businesses that deal in current cards and that of businesses that collect and sell historic cards.

2. Compare the expenses and profits of selling cards that you produce versus collecting and selling existing cards.

3. Compare the expenses and profits of businesses dealing in other memorabilia (e.g., old game programs, celebrity uniforms and equipment, autographs).

DUGOUT

It can pay to be a stockholder in a sports card business. Insiders in one company bought stock for 75¢ a share and sold it for $13 four years later. At 100,000 shares, what would be the profit?

The Gambling Life

TEACHER PLAY BOOK

☑ **ACTIVITY DESCRIPTION:** Students calculate the risks in sports gambling.

☑ **SPORTS:** All

☑ **MATHEMATICAL STRAND OUTCOMES:** Students will:
- calculate the odds of winning in sports events
- calculate the gambling economics of sports events
- represent data in graphic form

☑ **INFORMATION LITERACY OUTCOMES:** Students will:
- locate information on sports gambling
- identify key features in the gambling industry

☑ **PREREQUISITE SKILLS:**
- basic probability skills

☑ **RATIONALE FOR THE ACTIVITY:** Sometimes people think they can make more money gambling on sports than investing in them. This activity helps students realize the odds on sports gambling.

☑ **COACHING TIPS:** This is a fun activity for incorporating newspaper statistics.

From: *Go Figure! Mathematics Through Sports.* © 1999 Lesley S. J. Farmer. Teacher Ideas Press. 1-800-237-6124.

WARM-UPS

1. In New Jersey, 39,352 batting calls were made in 1994. Of the gamblers, 40% bet on sports and 30% bet on horse-racing. The average gambling debt was $25,151, and the gamblers' average annual income was $40,220. Three-quarters were male and half were married (the average family size was 2.9 children) (Siegel 1996, 37). What conclusions can you make from these data?

2. Probability odds are noted as 1:3 when there is one chance in three that an event will happen. In horse-racing, if a person bets $1 on those odds and the horse wins, the better gets $3—theoretically. In actuality, the figures are written as "3–1" and the lowest bet is $2, for which you might expect $8 ($6 on the odds and $2 for the original bet). Instead, the better gets $6.60 because the "house" typically gets 17% of the money to cover their expenses. Taking this percentage into mind, calculate the winnings on a $2 bet for the following odds: 6–1, 1–1, 4–5.

3. Consider tossing a penny. Even if it lands heads nine out of ten times, the next toss still has a fifty-fifty chance of landing heads. The same with betting; some players think they are "due" to win if they lose a lot. Actually, it makes more sense to bet more when winning and less when losing. Try the math for two different approaches:

    a. Gambler A decides how much he wants to win, and adjusts his wager after each bet (e.g., if he starts with $100 and wants to profit $50 but loses $20 in the first race, then he has to make $70 in the second race and thus bets more).

    b. Gambler B bets 5% of whatever capital he has (e.g., if he starts with $100, bets $20, and wins $50, then for the second race he would bet 5% of $130). Chart the difference in profits for two five-race scenarios by type A and type B betting approaches. Assume 5–2 odds (with returns as shown above), with each gambler starting with a $20 wager. In scenario A all horses win; in scenario B all horses lose.

158 The Gambling Life

STUDENT GAME PLAN

☑ **CONTEXT:** Maybe you're not the prime athlete, but you feel lucky and think you can make a bundle betting on sports competitions and events.

☑ **CHALLENGE:** Calculate the odds of winning on sports bets. Decide whether to become a sports gambler.

☑ **TASKS:**

1. Choose a sport that offers gambling options (e.g., horse-racing, football).
2. Research how the odds are figured in your sport. Factor in the house "take."
3. Produce a table that shows the probability of winning relative to your sport.
4. Analyze the data in terms of the likelihood of your becoming a profitable sports gambler.

☑ **RESOURCES:** Sources of information on sports events and gambling.

☑ **ASSESSMENT:** Your final project should consist of a table showing gambling odds and an analysis of the issues of sports gambling. You will be assessed on the accuracy and thoroughness of your data, the clarity of your data representations, and the logic of your argument.

☑ **STRETCHERS:**

1. Trace the history of sports gambling.
2. Compare the economics of on- and off-site betting.

DUGOUT

It costs at least $25,000 to maintain and train a thoroughbred horse for major competition. That doesn't count jockey costs. What do you estimate is the average income for a season of horse-racing?

$7,500. Of the horses, .04% get 5% of the purse money; another 3% account for 25% (Ainslie 1986, 73).

Marathon: Is Sports in Your Future?

TEACHER PLAY BOOK

☑ **ACTIVITY DESCRIPTION:** Students investigate sports careers.

☑ **SPORTS:** All

☑ **MATHEMATICAL STRAND OUTCOMES:** Students will:
- calculate investments and returns for sports careers
- incorporate percentages and probabilities into the data analysis
- represent data in spreadsheet and graphical form

☑ **INFORMATION LITERACY OUTCOMES:**
- locate information on sports careers
- determine significant factors in choosing a career

☑ **PREREQUISITE SKILLS:**
- basic spreadsheet skills

☑ **RATIONALE FOR THE ACTIVITY:** The probability that a student will become a star professional athlete is slim, but there are many lucrative and satisfying sports-related careers that students can explore.

☑ **COACHING TIPS:** Have students brainstorm sports-related careers. You might start by relating sports to each school department: sports statistician in math, physical therapist in science, sportswriter in English, team publicist in foreign languages, sports psychotherapist or marketer from social studies, sports trainer in P.E., sports illustrator in the arts, sports broadcaster or graphics designer in applied technology. Students also need help in identifying career factors: education, internships, networking, openings and outlook, room for advancement, continuing education, and special qualifications.

WARM-UPS

1. The minimum salary for a professional baseball player in 1947 was $5,000. In 1967 it was $6,000. In 1981, because of union negotiations, it was $40,000, and by 1990 it was $100,000. At that rate, what would be the minimum salary in 2000? Graph the change.

2. In 1996 there were about 38,000 recreational therapists, 42% in hospitals and 38% in nursing homes. What percentage would work in other settings?

   a. What is the actual number of recreational therapists in each setting?

   b. The average annual salary for a recreational therapist is $33,000; the average for recreational therapists in government positions is $39,400. If 25% of them are self-employed, do you think they would receive a higher or lower salary than a government worker?

STUDENT GAME PLAN

☑ **CONTEXT:** So you want to be the next Joe Montana. Are you willing to put in the time for preparation, promotion, and personal sacrifice? Do you understand that your career will be over before you hit your midlife crisis? What if you could make as much money over a lifetime as Joe Montana, but not be racked by physical pain? Consider a sports lawyer, a physician concentrating on sports injuries, a physical therapist, or a sports agent. Sound interesting?

☑ **CHALLENGE:** Investigate a sports-related career.

☑ **TASKS:**

1. Identify a sports-related career.

2. Research the career's qualifications, preparation, openings and outlook, opportunities for advancement, and salaries.

3. Derive mathematical evidence for the career. For instance, plot the net income (revenue minus expenditures) by year in order to represent the educational (and other) investment in the career. Make sure to include a cumulative profit margin for your career advancement. You may want to make a flowchart of career decisions.

☑ **RESOURCES:** Sources of information on sports careers (a good Web site is http://www.onlinesports.com/pages/CareerCenter.html); spreadsheet software or supplies.

☑ **ASSESSMENT:** Your final project should include your career plan, backed by mathematical evidence. You will be assessed on the thoroughness and logic of your plan and the justification of your career decisions.

☑ **STRETCHERS:**

1. Create a decision flowchart of possible careers.

2. Plot the relationship between career salary and probability of career choice.

DUGOUT

Who is football's highest-paid performer?

John Madden, who signed a $32 million, four-year deal in 1994.

Bibliography

MATH

Asimov, Isaac. *Realm of Measure*. Boston: Houghton Mifflin, 1960.

Cross, Wilbur. *Growing Your Small Business Made Simple*. New York: Doubleday, 1993.

Graphing Power. Palo Alto, Calif.: Dale Seymour Publications, 1995.

Harris, Robert. *Information Graphics*. Atlanta, Ga.: Maneyene Graphics, 1996.

Jacobs, Harold R. *Mathematics: A Human Endeavor*. San Francisco: W. H. Freeman, 1970.

Jacoby, Oswald. *How to Figure the Odds*. Garden City, N.Y.: Doubleday, 1947.

Joint Committee of the Mathematical Association of America and the National Council of Teachers of Mathematics. *A Sourcebook of Applications of School Mathematics*. Reston, Va.: National Council of Teachers of Mathematics, 1980.

Moore, David S., and George P. McCabe. *Introduction to the Practice of Statistics*. New York: W. H. Freeman, 1989.

Newman, J. *The World of Mathematics*. New York: Simon & Schuster, 1956.

Polya, George. *How to Solve It*. Princeton, N.J.: Princeton University Press, 1988.

Stenmark, Jean Kerr, Virginia Thompson, and Ruth Cossey. *Family Math*. Berkeley: University of California Press, 1986.

Used Numbers. Palo Alto, Calif.: Dale Seymour Publications, 1992.

Van Der Meer, Ron, and Bob Gardner. *The Math Kit*. New York: Macmillan, 1994.

Vorderman, Carol. *How Math Works*. Pleasantville, N.Y.: Reader's Digest Association, 1996.

ANATOMY AND FITNESS

The Encyclopedia of Health. New York: Chelsea House, 1990– .

Goodhart, R. *Modern Nutrition in Health and Disease*. Philadelphia: Lea & Febiger, 1980.

Kirschmann, Gayla J., and John D. Kirschmann. *Nutrition Almanac*. 4th ed. New York: McGraw-Hill, 1996.

Kittredge, Mary. *The Human Body: An Overview*. New York: Chelsea House, 1990.

Knapp, Rebecca Grant. *Basic Statistics for Nurses*. New York: John Wiley, 1978.

Lindsay, Robert Bruce. *Introduction to Physical Statistics*. New York: Dover Publications, 1941.

Loomis, Andrew. *Figure Drawing*. New York: Viking Press, 1946.

Parker, Steve. *How the Body Works*. Pleasantville, N.Y.: Reader's Digest Association, 1994.

PDR Family Guide to Nutrition and Health. Montvale, N.J.: Medical Economics, 1995.

Southmayd, William, and Marshall Hoffman. *Sports Health*. New York: G. P. Putnam's Sons, 1981.

Sprague, Ken. *The Athlete's Body*. Boston: Houghton Mifflin, 1981.

Stonehouse, Bernard. *The Way Your Body Works*. New York: Crown, 1974.

University of California, Berkeley. Student Health Service and the Department of Physical Education. *Fitness and Health Handbook*. Champaign, Ill.: Life Enhancement Publications, 1985.

SCIENCE

Cassidy, John. *Explorabook*. Palo Alto, Calif.: Klutz Press, 1991.

Freeman, Ira. *Physics Made Simple*. Rev. ed. New York: Doubleday, 1990.

Hann, Judith. *How Science Works*. Pleasantville, N.Y.: Reader's Digest Association, 1991.

Jensen, Clayne R., and Gordon W. Schultz. *Applied Kinesiology*. New York: McGraw-Hill, 1977.

Macaulay, David. *The Way Things Work*. Boston: Houghton Mifflin, 1988.

Morton, Richard F., and J. Richard Hebel. *A Study Guide to Epidemiology and Biostatistics*. Baltimore, Md.: University Park Press, 1979.

Ricci, Benjamin. *Physiological Basis of Human Performance*. Philadelphia: Lea & Febiger, 1967.

Ultimate Visual Dictionary of Science. London: Dorling Kindersley, 1998.

Weyl, Peter K. *Men, Ants and Elephants*. New York: Viking, 1959.

SPORTS

Ainslie, Tom. *Ainslie's Complete Guide to Thoroughbred Racing*. New York: Simon & Schuster, 1986.

Brancazio, Peter J. *Sport Science*. New York: Simon & Schuster, 1984.

———. *Sports Figures*. Bristol, Conn.: ESPN, 1997.

Broido, Bing. *Spalding Book of Rules*. Indianapolis, Ind.: Howard W. Sams, 1993.

Brunner, Borgna, ed. *Information Please Almanac 1998*. Boston: Information Please, 1997.

Chase, Sara B. *Moving to Win: The Physics of Sports*. New York: Julian Messner, 1977.

Coffland, Jack, and David A. Coffland. *Football Math*. Glenview, Ill.: GoodYearBooks, 1995.

Davis, Susan, Sally Stephens, and the Exploratorium. *The Sporting Life*. New York: Henry Holt, 1997.

Diagram Group. *The Rule Book*. New York: St. Martin's Press, 1983.

Dickson, Paul. *The Joy of Keeping Score*. New York: Walker, 1996.

Farber, Michael. "Try These on for Cys." *Sports Illustrated,* Sept. 14, 1998, pp. 36–42.

Fischler, Stan, et al. *20th Century Hockey Chronicle*. Lincolnwood, Ill.: Publications International, 1994.

Gorman, Jerry, and Kirk Calhoun. *The Name of the Game*. New York: John Wiley, 1994.

Kettelkamp, Larry. *Modern Sports Science*. New York: William Morrow, 1986.

Kraemer, William J., and Steven J. Fleck. *Strength Training for Young Athletes*. Windsor, Ont.: Human Kinetics, 1993.

Levinson, David, and Karen Christensen, eds. *Encyclopedia of World Sport*. Santa Barbara, Calif.: ABC-CLIO, 1997.

McGraw, Dan. "Big League Troubles." *U.S. News & World Report,* July 13, 1998, pp. 40–46.

Meserole, Mike, ed. *1995 Information Please Sports Almanac*. Boston: Houghton Mifflin, 1995.

Rosenzweig, Sandra. *Sportsfitness for Women*. New York: Harper & Row, 1982.

Siegel, M., N. Jacobs, and S. Landes. *Gambling: Crime or Recreation?* Wylie, Tex.: Information Plus, 1996.

"Sosa & McGwire." *Time,* Sept. 14, 1998, p. 22.

Sports Shorts. Palo Alto, Calif.: Dale Seymour Publications, 1987.

Sugar, Bert Randolph. *Baseballistics*. New York: St. Martin's Press, 1990.

Watts, Robert G., and A. Terry Bahill. *Keep Your Eye on the Ball*. New York: W. H. Freeman, 1990.

Williams, Pete. *Card Sharks*. New York: Macmillan, 1995.

Williams, Ted, and John Underwood. *The Science of Hitting*. New York: Simon & Schuster, 1971.

Yogt, Sharon. *Olympic Math*. Glenview, Ill.: GoodYearBooks, 1996.

Young, Mark, ed. *The Guinness Book of Sports Records, 1992*. New York: Facts on File, 1992.

Zumerchik, John, ed. *Encyclopedia of Sports Science*. New York: Macmillan, 1997.

INSTRUCTION

Adrini, B. *Cooperative Learning and Math: A Multi-Structural Approach*. San Juan Capistrano, Calif.: Resources for Teachers, 1989.

American Association of School Librarians and Association for Educational Communications and Technology. *Information Power: Building Partnerships for Learning*. Chicago: American Library Association, 1998.

Boober, Becky Hayes, Jacqueline P. Mitchell, and Caroll Jordan Hatcher. *Measuring Up in Mathematics*. Duvall, Wash: CJHatcher & Associates, 1992.

Brooks, J. G., and M. G. Brooks. *In Search of Understanding: The Case for Constructivist Classrooms*. Alexandria, Va.: Association for Supervision and Curriculum Development, 1993.

Costa, A., and R. Liebmann. *Envisioning Process as Content: Towards Renaissance Curriculum*. Thousand Oaks, Calif.: Corwin Press, 1996.

Davidson, N. *Cooperative Learning in Mathematics: A Handbook for Teachers*. Reading, Mass.: Addison-Wesley, 1989.

Farmer, Lesley S. J. *Cooperative Learning in the Library Media Center*. Rev. ed. Englewood, Colo.: Libraries Unlimited, 1999.

Gardner, H. *Multiple Intelligences: The Theory in Practice*. New York: Basic Books, 1993.

Harmin, Merrill. *Inspiring Active Learning: A Handbook for Teachers*. Alexandria, Va.: Association for Supervision and Curriculum Development, 1994.

Improving Science and Mathematics Education: A Database and Catalog of Alternative Assessments. 3d ed. Portland, Ore.: Northwest Regional Educational Laboratory, n.d.

Interactive Mathematics Activities and Investigations. New York: McGraw-Hill, 1995.

Introduction and Implementation Strategies for the Interactive Mathematics Program. Berkeley, Calif.: Key Curriculum Press, 1998.

Johnson, D. W., and R. T. Johnson. *Learning Together and Alone*. 4th ed. Needham Heights, Mass.: Allyn & Bacon, 1997.

Kagan, Spencer. *Cooperative Learning Structures*. Rev. ed. San Juan Capistrano, Calif.: Kagan Cooperative Learning, 1992.

Mathematics Framework for California Public Schools. Sacramento: California Department of Education, 1992.

National Council of Teachers of Mathematics. *Assessment Standards Working Groups. Assessment Standards for School Mathematics*. Reston, Va.: National Council of Teachers of Mathematics, 1995.

———. Commission on Standards for School Mathematics. *Curriculum and Evaluation Standards for School Mathematics*. Reston, Va.: National Council of Teachers of Mathematics, 1989.

———. Commission on Teaching Standards for School Mathematics. *Professional Standards for Teaching Mathematics*. Reston, Va.: National Council of Teachers of Mathematics, 1991.

———. "Principles and Standards for Schools." Draft. Reston, Va.: National Council of Teachers of Mathematics, 1998.

Oregon Museum of Science and Industry. *Teacher's Guide Star Trek Federation Science*. Boston: Science Network, 1992.

Sharan, S., and Y. Haran. *Expanding Cooperative Learning Through Group Investigation*. New York: Teachers College Press, 1992.

Index

academic preparation, 3
accounting, 133, 136, 140
advertisements, 27
aerobic exercise, 61
Ainslie, Tom, 158
air resistance, 84, 86
amateur athletes, 122, 136
American Association of School Librarians, 12
American Library Association, 12
anabolic improvement, 55
anaerobic exercise, 61
area, 71
Asimov, Isaac, 32
assessment of work, xiv, 4, 7-8, 12
attention, students', 4
authenticity, 4
auto racing, 85, 134

Bannister, Roger, 105
Barbie doll, 26
Basal Metabolic Rate (BMR), 52, 53
baseball, 74, 87, 95, 98, 104, 110, 111, 117, 121, 126, 139, 153, 160
basketball, 61, 72, 82, 120, 130, 151
Bernoulli's Principle, 84, 85
bias, 107, 143
blood, 34, 39
body composition, 33
body conditioning, 67
body image, 21, 25
Body Mass Index (BMI), 30
bowling, 65, 73
broad jump records, 32

CAD software, 86
calculators, 122
California Department of Education, 6
calories, 49, 52, 61
cardiac output, 61
cards, sports, 152-155
careers, 159
chart format, 109

classification of information, 106
climbing, 141
coaching, 13
collision, force of, in sports, 78
combinations, sports, 74, 119
communication, 7, 8
competitions, 126, 128
conditioning, body, 67
content analysis, 108
cooperation, 13
correlation, 51, 60, 67, 103, 116, 125
cubit, 22
curling, 65
curriculum, 3, 6, 7, 11
cycling, 61, 89

daily life, 4
data gathering, 10
database record, 40
density, 31
design brief, 9
diagnosis, 40
diagrams, 58, 64, 84, 91, 97
diet, 48
Diet Center, 55
disease, 66
drugs, 66
dugout sections, defined, 15

eccentricity, 95
economics, 133, 135, 138, 140, 143, 152-55
energy, 78, 80, 96
equipment, sports, 84, 94, 96
equity, 8
ESPN sports coverage, 106
exercise, 48, 60, 61
experiments, 10, 94
experimentation, mathematical model for, 10, 94

facilities, 140, 144
Farber, Michael, 126
fat, 34, 52, 55
fields, playing, 71

fitness/training, 31, 67, 140
foot (measure), 23
football, 75, 112, 120, 127, 129, 137, 144, 148, 150
force, 56, 58, 64, 78, 90, 91, 94
formula, physics, 91
framework, 15
franchises, sports, 140, 143
friction, 92, 93
functions, 15, 63, 64, 67

gambling, 156, 157, 158
game plan, 17
games, 10, 76
gaming theory, 10, 11
gears, 89
gender, 34, 35, 49, 106, 134
geometry, 15, 71
girls, and math, xiii
golf, 85, 87, 110
Goodhart, R., 49
graphs, 63, 78, 81, 103, 109, 116, 133, 146, 149, 152, 156, 159
gravity, 82, 95

habits of mind, 3, 7
hammer throw, 89
hand, as measure of length, 22
handball, 137
health, 40, 43, 54
heat, 39
heuristics, 9
hitting, 96
hockey, 92, 115
hormones, 55
horsepower, 57
horseracing, 134, 157
hypermedia, 42
hypothesis, 10, 27, 113, 123

inclusion of all students in learning, 5
individual sports, 109, 135
inference, 25, 32, 122, 129
information literacy, xiv, 12, 13
injury, 64, 66
instructional design and implementation, 8, 9
Interactive Physics software, 56, 64, 66

Internet, 55, 128
investigation, 11
Jenny Craig, 55
jogging, 65

King John of England, 23

labor, 146
lean body mass (LBM), 52
learning environment, 4
learning style, 3, 5, 7, 11
levers, 56
lift, 84
library media teacher, 13
Loomis, Andrew, 28

machines, 56, 58
marathon activities, 15, 16
Markov chains, 119
mass, 31
Mathematica, 12
mathematical model for experimentation, 10, 94
matrix, 125
McGraw, Dan, 144
measurement, 12, 21-43
mechanics, 64, 88
media, 107, 144, 161
metabolism, 36
mind, habits of, 3, 7
momentum, 79
Monte Carlo simulations, 11
Morceli, Moureddine, 105
motion, 58, 88
multimedia, 97

National Collegiate Athletic Association, 137
National Council of Teachers of Mathematics (NCTM), xiv, 5, 6, 10
Newman, J., 32
Nutri-System, 55
nutrition, 47, 48, 49, 50

officiation, 113, 115
Olympics, 57, 62, 108, 130, 147
oscillation, 95

PDR, 54
percentage, 47, 51, 159
perimeter, 71
permutations, 42
physics, 56, 67, 91
physiology, 15, 21, 25, 29, 33, 37, 47, 51
pie chart, 35, 49, 54, 147
play book, 16
playground, 65
playing fields, 71
Polya, George, 9
population, 25, 122
portfolios, 4, 7
power, 56
prediction, 103, 109, 140, 143, 149
probability, 128, 152, 156, 157, 159
professionals, 122
projectiles, 81
proportion, 27
protein, 48

racquetball, 72
ratio, 51
Recommended Dietary Allowance, 48
records, 103
recreational therapy, 160
regression analysis, 103, 125, 143
Ricci, Benjamin, 39
rotation, 88
rotational force, 90
rote learning, 3
rowing, 123
rubrics, 8
rugby, 65

sampling, 27
Sargent jump, 31
SCANS report, xiii
scatterplot, 29, 71, 104
scheduling, 121
scores, 74, 118
sequencing, 103
shoes, 91
shuttlecock, 82
simulation, 11, 128
skating, 89, 92, 114, 148

soccer, 117, 147
sociogram, 146
span, as measure of length, 22
special education, 7
Special Olympics, 147
sports, 13, 15
sports cards, 152, 161-65
sports equipment, 84, 94, 96
sports franchises, 140, 143
sports training techniques, 13
spreadsheet, 50, 51, 108, 133, 136, 149, 152, 159
statistics, 15, 25, 64, 103, 106, 109, 113, 122, 125, 149, 152
stretcher activities, defined, 15
Sugar, Bert Randolph, 104
surveys, 10, 11, 25
sweat, 48, 61
sweet spot, 95
swimming, 77
symbols, 11
systems
    English, 24
    metric, 24
    Système International (SI), 24

tables, data, 113, 122, 128
teachers, what they need to know, 11
teams, 121, 125, 128, 138, 143, 145, 149, 151
technology, 9, 11, 12
tennis, 95, 129, 134
throwing, 83, 89, 124
timing, 116
torque, 64, 65, 95
track, 61, 105
trajectory, 81
trigonometry, 94
training, 15, 54, 58, 68
training techniques, 13

variables, 60, 103, 122
variance statistical procedures, 122
vectors, 56, 64, 81, 88, 94
velocity, 56, 85
vibration, 95
volume, 71

warm-up activities, defined, 15, 16
water loss and requirements, 39, 48
weight, 48, 52
Weight Watchers, 54
wheels, 88, 90
Williams, Pete, 154
Williams, Ted, 153

work (physics), 57
workout activities, defined, 15, 16
wrestling, 79

yearbook, 108
YMCA, 142

Zumerchik, John, 92

About the Author

Dr. Lesley Farmer, Library Media Teacher Services Credential Program Coordinator, is associate professor of Library Media Technology at California State University Long Beach. Officer and frequent presenter at state and national library and technology conferences, Dr. Farmer has published a dozen books on librarianship, and has edited several professional publications. In addition, she has garnered several professional awards, the most recent being the 1999 Region IV CTAP (California Technology Assistance Program) Instructional Technology Award and the 1998 CSLA Technology Award. Dr. Farmer received her M.S.L.S. from the University of North Carolina at Chapel Hill and her doctorate from Temple University. She has worked in both public and private school library settings, special and government libraries, as well as academic and public libraries.

from Teacher Ideas Press

FAMOUS PROBLEMS AND THEIR MATHEMATICIANS
Art Johnson

How did fly paper lead to a new field in mathematics? Why did ordering an omelette cost one mathematician his life? Find the answers in this exciting resource that makes math more relevant to the average student. Johnson walks students through the solutions for more than 60 math problems and then applies the solutions to everyday situations. Reproducibles, historical facts, and extension activities fill in the big picture. **Grades 5–12**.
ca180p. 8½x11 paper ISBN 1-56308-446-5

CIVIC MATHEMATICS
Fundamentals in the Context of Social Issues
Terry Vatter

"What has math got to do with my life?" If you've ever heard that protest from your students, this book may provide the answer. Presenting mathematics in the context of social issues makes it relevant and helps students learn how to apply math skills appropriately. **Grades 6–10**.
xvi, 169p. 8½x11 paper ISBN 1-56308-435-X

ART IN CHEMISTRY; CHEMISTRY IN ART
Barbara R. Greenberg and Dianne Patterson

With more than 60 hands-on activities and a number of fascianting demonstrations, this book enables students to see and understand how the science of chemistry is involoved in the creation of art. Topics include color paint, supports and grounds, clay, sculpture and organic chemistry, jewelry, photography, and art forgery. **Grades 7–12** (adaptable to other levels).
xiv, 259p. 8½x11 paper ISBN 1-56308-487-2

MARVELS OF MATH
Fascinating Reads and Awesome Activities
Kendall Haven

Show students how dynamic mathematics really is with the riveting stories and intriguing facts found here! Haven offers 16 dramatic accounts of the innovations and triumphs of mathematicians throughout history. Accompanying each story are terms to learn, discussion questions, and activities and experiments that amplify the story's theme. **Grades 3–9**.
xii, 172p. 6x9 paper ISBN 1-56308-585-2

THE SCIENCE AND MATH BOOKMARK BOOK
Kendall Haven and Roni Berg

Get the basics of math and science across with 300 bookmarks designed to interest and inform your students. With simple language and dynamic graphics, the bookmarks stimulate thinking and reinforce lessons with quizzes, key scientist profiles, and much more! **Grades 1–6**.
xii, 115p. 8½x11 paper ISBN 1-56308-675-1

For a FREE catalog or to place an order, please contact:

Teacher Ideas Press
Dept. B921 · P.O. Box 6633 · Englewood, CO 80155-6633
1-800-237-6124, ext. 1 · Fax: 303-220-8843 · E-mail: lu-books@lu.com

 **Check out the TIP Web site!**
www.lu.com/tip

www.ingramcontent.com/pod-product-compliance
Lightning Source LLC
Chambersburg PA
CBHW080551230426
43663CB00015B/2790